ALL PATHS LEAD TO PURPOSE

PHILLIP E. GRAHAM, PH.D.

KP PUBLISHING COMPANY

ISBN: 978-1-960001-71-9 (Paperback)
ISBN: 978-1-960001-72-6 (Ebook)

Library of Congress: 2024908215

Editor/Proofreader: Manuscript Mender, LLC
Cover Design: Juan Roberts, Creative Lunacy
Literary Director: Sandra Slayton James

Published by:

KP Publishing Company
Publisher of Fiction, Nonfiction & Children's Books
Las Vegas, NV 89117
www.kp-pub.com

Printed in the United States of America

DEDICATION

This book is respectfully dedicated to everyone on the path to discovering their purpose.

May your journey be joyous and filled with many adventures.

To my late mother, Kathy D. Graham, the first person to believe in me. I hope to forever be the embodiment of the dreams you had for me.

To my late grandfather, Samuel J. Graham, a man who has been a pillar in my life and development. Who would often say, "If you're pushing others to the top, you can't be too far behind."

To my grandmother, siblings, and everyone who has supported me along this journey, this book is written in your honor.

And to the late Dr. Troy J. Shine. A friend's friend. May you find rest and peace knowing you fulfilled your purpose in this life.

CONTENTS

Contents

INTRODUCTION

"The path to our destination is not always a straight one.
We go down the wrong road, we get lost, we turn back.
Maybe it doesn't matter which road we embark on.
Maybe what matters is that we embark."

—BARBARA HALL

This quotation from author and television producer Barbara Hall is the embodiment of this book dedicated to those who are seeking purpose. Hall's words suggest that no matter the path or direction we take, it will eventually lead to discovering our mission in life. We need only to start the journey, make our intentions clear, and listen to "the omens," as *The Alchemist* author, Paul Coelho, tells us. Walk the path that is before you and create the opportunities that you wish to have. Nothing is off-limits. We are only limited by the restrictions that we place on ourselves—the lack of imagination, negative thinking, or failure to launch.

This book is written and respectfully dedicated to any and every one of you embarking on a path to finding your true purpose. Those of you who are diligently seeking your *raison d'etre*, the reason for being, and how to clearly identify it. Allow this work to help illuminate your path. Each chapter will touch on a few of the things I have identified that relate to finding purpose. Use what you can and add your own experiences to the list. Purpose extends beyond the borders of these passages and reaches into the depth of our very existence. I am writing this book with the intention of finding my own purpose and helping others discover theirs along the way.

I invite you to read this with an open mind and take the same approach to anything and everything that you read or watch as it relates to discovering your purpose. In the book *Mindset*, author Carol S. Dweck informs us that the way we think about a situation can drastically change the outcome of the event. I strongly recommend that you read it, especially if you tend to have a pessimistic disposition. For the duration of your journey, I encourage you to tap into the parts of you that are eagerly hopeful, optimistic, and flexible. A major part of discovering your purpose is by letting go of a rigid and fixed mentality.

If you have happened upon this book, it means you are on the right path. Your internal desire to answer the age-old mystery of life is beginning to unfold! Keep walking, and eventually, it will become clear. Depending on where you are in life, if you are anything like me, at times, you will feel lost. That feeling may be a scary and isolated experience, especially if those around you seem to be on a sure path.

Fret not, because "not all who wander are lost" (J.R.R. Tolkien). Hopefully, this book will help lead you one step closer to finding purpose. Allow yourself to maintain your sense of wonder and learn to reach into the deep recesses of your mind to discover self and the meaning of life. Most importantly, remember to keep in mind: All Paths Lead to Purpose.

CHAPTER 1

THE PRICE

"What I think is there's no shortcut, ever, for anyone.
Life teaches us this lesson. There are no shortcuts,
and if you get it really quickly you pay a little bit later.

—Diane Von Furstenberg: Unracked

As you begin this journey, I want to caution you about events that are sure to take place in your life as a result of pursuing your purpose. If you are truly serious about attaining this goal, heed this warning from the famous 19th-century British author Charles Dickens: "The important thing is this: to be ready at any moment to sacrifice what you are for what you could become." When you pursue your purpose, you might discover that you have more clarity of mind or that you've lost every friend you ever had. Beware, your pursuit may cost you everything—but the price you pay does not compare to the reward. As Dickens warns, we must remain steadfast and ready to give up all that we know or think we know in order to become what we are to become. One of the primary things that hinders us along our journey is the notion that the things we want come without sacrifice.

With a clear mind and open to the possibilities of what lies ahead, understand up front that nothing is freely given. In economics, we learn that "there is no such thing as a free lunch." This is a well-known adage that reflects a universal truth: everything comes at a cost, even purpose. Damilola Oluwatoyinbo states, "Too many people want to have mountaintop experiences at rock-bottom prices, and that just doesn't work. Greatness doesn't come at a discount. If you want true greatness, you have to pay the full price for it." Many people make this common mistake: they are not fully invested and not willing to pay the cost. These are the people that you will find spinning in circles, stuck in the same place of perpetual torment. Never moving forward, they feel entitled and bitter, and they never understand why they remain stagnant. They are eventually propelled into a never-ending existential crisis, wandering, lost in a befuddled space of not knowing why things never seem to work out. They want all the rewards with none of the risk; unfortunately, life just doesn't work like that. We can all admit that we have found ourselves in that position, a time or two.

The important thing is that we recognize our shortcomings and adjust our actions when we gain awareness.

The truth of the matter is every person of note has "paid the price"—and as I write, I reflect on the life of the late Nelson Mandela. We remember his legacy and may negate the fact that he spent 27 years in prison in order to fulfill his purpose and, ultimately, his destiny. Not only did that destiny cost him his freedom, comfort, and sanity, it also cost him his family, love, and more than we may possibly imagine. We all want to leave that kind of impact on the world, but are we willing to pay the price? I use Mandela as an example, but if you read or know of the stories of anyone that you admire, they all pay a price. If you are a religious person, you might think of the ultimate price Jesus paid for those who believe in him. Others might think about Mahatma Gandhi, Albert Einstein, and countless others. These people will forever live on in the annals of time because they understood (the assignment) that the risk was worth the reward.

The universe requires a sacrifice because it is a sign that you are equally committed to fulfilling your purpose, and your sacrifice is the dowry. The cosmos is funny that way; it may appear that some people are required to pay little to nothing for the gifts they receive, while others seem to pay the ultimate price for seemingly little gain. In a conversation I had with a great friend on a recent trip to New York City, he told me that as it relates to our purpose, we all pay the price. Some people, he said, pay upfront, and others pay later, but we all pay. He was quoting something he heard in a movie, but the sentiment resonated with me. The universe is not naïve, nor is it forgetful; everyone will eventually pay what's due. It merely operates on the wavelength of expedience.

I believe that there is a grand scheme and master plan laid out by the powers in the universe. Not to suggest that we are without free will because I also believe in the principle of free will; if this were not the case, then this book would be meaningless. However, as it pertains to purpose, some people have been destined to fulfill a role that only they can satisfy. They are still required to pay a price, as no one is exempt from this debt.

Nonetheless, this much should be clear: when the time comes, the opportunity presents itself, and the bill becomes due; are you willing and able to pay the price? If your answer is no, it may be best for you to stop here. There is no point in pursuing your purpose any further if you are not willing to offer up whatever you are asked to relinquish. The universe offers us a choice in this matter, but we must learn to distinguish its voice and what it requires of us. If you choose to continue, then you are continuing on the path—and by the end of this book, you will be several steps closer to finding and discovering your purpose.

PURPOSE COMES FREELY

According to The Free Dictionary, purpose is defined as:

Purpose: (pûr′pəs) *n.*

1. The object toward which one strives or for which something exists; an aim or goal: Her purpose in coming here is to talk to you. The purpose of an airliner is to transport people. See Synonyms at intention.

2. Determination; resolution: He was a man of purpose. *tr.v.* **purposed, pur·pos·ing, purposes** To intend or resolve: "the gap between what is said and what is purposed" (Ian Donaldson). **Idioms:** *on purpose;* Intentionally; deliberately; *to*

4

good purpose; With good results; *to little/no
purpose;*
With few or no results.

I believe that it's important to take a step back before we move forward. I fundamentally and unequivocally believe that we were all created with purpose and on purpose. Our *raison d'etre* is why we were brought into existence in this place, at this time. This "reason for being" transcends circumstances, vocation, and resources. We were shaped, molded, and created intentionally, but it is ultimately up to us what we do with the gift of life that has been bestowed upon us. The reason for one's existence comes without cost. To be, to exist, to think freely, to love, to laugh, to hurt, to cry—these are gifts given to us with no strings attached. There is no price to pay for just being, depending on how you look at it.

Whether or not we find and or fulfill our purpose is completely up to us. The quest takes me back to the days of long conversations with my parents about "living up to my potential." As I was growing up, there were countless examples at arm's length of people who never quite achieved their goals in life. This begs the question, are some people destined for a life of unfulfilled potential? Could their purpose be only to serve as an example of what not to do, be, or become? That may or may not be the case; nonetheless, I believe some people fall victim to circumstances, and the pitfalls in their lives can be so discouraging that it pulls them away from their purpose. When our life steers off course in a way that we cannot connect to, we exhibit feelings of fear and anxiety, not realizing that no matter the place or course in life that we veer off on, the totality of our journey leads us to our ultimate destination.

This brings us here. If you are reading this book, it's because your purpose may seem unclear. As the French essayist Michel de Montaigne writes, "The soul which has no fixed purpose in life is lost; to be everywhere is to be nowhere." You may have been drawn to this book because you are stuck in the foggy mist of doubt and uncertainty. Your mission is to discover why you were placed here and how to move steadfastly along that path.

> Because, plainly put, purpose defines who we are and what we do in life. Think about it. We all know people who have a kind of inner glow—not because they eat a kale salad, but because they are animated by purpose. It feeds their self-worth. It informs their actions and helps them thoughtfully decide how and where they allocate energy. And that creates lives that are worth getting out of bed for. Discovering our purpose happens in different ways. Some see it in a sudden flash. For others, it comes more gradually: Stepping outside social norms or recovering from tragedy, or connecting with those less well-off. Then there are people who have always known what to do, either through family influence, passion, or instinct. No matter the course, when we realize our purpose, we realize what's fun about life.
>
> —Unstuck

Those who discover their purpose find fulfillment and the keys to success. A sense of purpose is built into the fabric of our DNA, and our primary obligation is to go in search of it and discover what it is. It is not so elusive that it is out of our reach; it only requires that we dig deep within ourselves and usher it out through actions. Purpose is a sentient being within our inner self, begging to be discovered, raging within us, seeping through our pores, and haunting us in our dreams. If we fail to discover it, we fail ourselves because the universe has made it so easy for us to find. We need only search the depths of our souls and bring it to fruition.

The concept is simple enough, but it is often the simple things in life that we overcomplicate. Some would say it's the simple things that confound the wise. My father would often say that gifts are given freely, and if you have to beg for a gift, then it's no gift at all. The gift is given freely, but we must put in some effort to identify it. Purpose resides within us rent-free; operating on it comes at a cost.

As a psychotherapist, I see countless clients who present with symptoms of anxiety, depression, and lack of motivation. They all sit before me and confess to being lost in life, with a deep desire to know why they exist. When asked about knowing their purpose, they all say that they are waiting to discover what it is. Life circumstances, however, have taught them to be afraid to move forward. They feel as if every decision they have made has only led to chaos, destruction, loneliness, and feeling disconnected. I surmise that the separation from purpose is a primary contributor to these mental health concerns. As a result, these individuals learned to stand still, play safe, and never rock the boat. Meanwhile, their purpose is creating a storm inside of them, urging them to move forward. Being stagnant, they suffer in silence, and the winds of purpose sent to set their sails instead turn inward, causing them to feel anxious, panicked, and displaced. To which I reply, "All paths lead to purpose. You just have to choose a path and walk it."

THE FAUSTIAN BARGAIN

What is the cost of your soul?

The legend of the revered blues musician, Robert Johnson, is one illustration of a "deal with the devil." Various iterations of this Faustian deal can be found in folklore and literature throughout the world. The stories relate how a seemingly ordinary person of little significance or talent suddenly attains the impossible and performs major feats of greatness overnight. The protagonist's wishes are granted beyond their wildest dreams. They experience the heights of greatness until the "bill comes due" and they must pay the price for their undue success. Suddenly, everything goes horribly wrong and comes crashing down in a blaze of shame and humiliation, and they realize that they sacrificed their very soul for momentary gratification.

The story of Robert Johnson goes like this:

> According to legend, as a young man living on a plantation
> in rural Mississippi, Johnson had a tremendous desire to
> become a great blues musician. He was instructed to take
> his guitar to a crossroad near Dockery Plantation at

8

midnight. There he was met by a large black man (the devil), who took the guitar and tuned it. The devil played a few songs and then returned the guitar to Johnson, giving him mastery of the instrument. This was a deal with the devil mirroring the legend of Faust. In exchange for his soul, Johnson was able to create the blues for which he became famous. Far Out Magazine, Tom Taylor, January 2021

What is the price of your soul? Is the value so little that you would trade in what's most precious to you for pebbles? Take your mind to a place where you seemingly have life figured out. You have some measure of success, money in your bank account, respect from friends and family, and perceived happiness. Everything is going well until one small thing unravels everything in your universe. Before you know it, you are back at step one. It's the starting over that shakes the foundation of your core, challenging your inner strength and destroying your confidence. You find yourself once again propelled into a desert of uncertainty and doubt. The longer we stay in that place, the longer and harder it is to leave. It is in these moments when all seems hopeless that some people are willing to go to great lengths that compromise their morality. Unscrupulous behaviors may pay off for some, but I'm an avid believer that they will eventually have to pay a cosmic toll because no one cheats the universe.

The installments paid for purpose cost whatever amount of work you are willing to put into it. It is to our own detriment that we take the easy way out because the easy path seldom works out in the end. If this is the path that you wish to take, you must understand fully that you are building your dreams on a shaky foundation that will lead you down a path to ruin.

As you walk along the path toward your destiny, you have to ask yourself this important question: What cup will I drink from? Will I indulge in a fantasy where hopes and aspirations go to die on a branch? Or linger in a constant state of what-ifs? Will I decide to act and hope for the best? Or to drink from a well of desire, salted by the tears of regrets that slowly kill from dehydration?

PAYING IT FORWARD

As we continue to sojourn on this road towards purpose, there are some things that should be made explicitly clear at this point. The purpose that you discover may not be intended to benefit you. Purpose, at its core, is intended to benefit the masses. It just happens that the extraordinary work of the individual *may* grant one fame and fortune. However, one's intentions should not be to seek superficial treasures. When the purpose is revealed, it often comes with sacrifice. The reward may be to help others achieve a goal that neglects to mention your name in the history books. If that were to be the case, would you still wish to follow this path?

Mason Wartman runs a pizza shop in Philadelphia appropriately named Wartman's. In an effort to help out homeless people in the city, which is a serious issue, he hatched a plan to allow customers to spend an extra dollar to prepay for a slice of pizza, then put a Post-It on the wall. Homeless people could then redeem the Post-It for a free slice, and as of February, the restaurant had given away more than 10,000 slices of pizza. NPR, Elizabeth Fiedler, January 2015

This story is the epitome of what it means to pay it forward. Some individuals are unable to fathom the concept of working hard without acknowledgment or compensation. So, they may ask themselves, then why seek it out? Well, it depends. Imagine for a moment that the minor role you must play contributes to the overall cosmic design, knowing that you were ultimately created to help the universe and that the universe wouldn't survive without your contribution. Imagine how powerful that is, knowing your life's purpose is intimately intertwined with the universe. No, you may not see the return on your investment in a traditional sense. However, the soul is repaid in ways that provide ultimate fulfillment and give meaning to one's very existence. The people who discover this are the people who can wake up satisfied with themselves. Money does not affect their mood, and negativity cannot live in the atmosphere they create for themselves. Great things may come as a result, but that should never be your aim. Set your sights on walking towards the path that you wish to travel and set it ablaze.

Years ago, a movie called *Pay it Forward* with a young Haley Joel Osment became an unconventional hit that turned into a movement. People began to grasp the concept that they should share the fruits of their bounty. Rather than hoard the generosity bestowed upon them, they will pass the blessing along in the hopes that it could touch everyone in the world, not only spreading the milk of human kindness but communicating that we are all interconnected somehow. Purpose can also operate as a network of the universe's intentions carried out by those who occupy it. After the movie hit the theaters, hundreds of stories of random acts of kindness began to spread, and the idea of *#payitforward* went viral.

It is my belief that if we are to be content in life, we must accept our purpose and execute it with humility, thankfulness, and grace. This is proof positive that we are spiritually mature and ready to embrace whatever other blessings flow our way. Emotional and spiritual maturity may determine how purpose is delegated and flows through us.

Things to consider:
- Purpose is free but not without a cost.
- The sacrifices are payments that ensure our commitment.
- There are no shortcuts to seeking purpose; trying to shortcut the process only leads to turmoil and destruction.
- Our purpose extends beyond us. Without reward or acknowledgment, we play a silent vital role in the universe's grand design.
- When we prove that we are spiritually and emotionally mature, we are endowed with a greater sense of purpose that may reach greater depths than we can conceive.

Path-to-Purpose Exercise:

Write a list of things you can think of that may apply to this section:

1. _____

2. _____

3. _____

4. _____

5. _____

CHAPTER 2

THE PURSUIT

"There are no mistakes in life, only lessons. There is no such thing as a negative experience, only opportunities to grow, learn, and advance along the road of self-mastery. From struggle comes strength. Even pain can be a wonderful teacher."

—Robin Sharma

Life is purposeful. The only task we have in living is to discover our purpose and pursue it relentlessly. The stars are aligned with purpose; they illuminate the night sky and create an atmosphere for lovers to find each other. Everything is orchestrated with purpose because the universe is intentional in its design. To that end, there are no mistakes in life. Everything we do, every heartache we feel, every win, and every loss were intended to add texture to the fabric of our individual stories. Take a moment to reflect on the hero's journey. The protagonist often prevails after a major feat. If these heroes were to never overcome the hardships, they would never reach the pinnacle of success and discover the courage to move forward toward their mission.

People often complain about the hardships they've had to endure in life because those hardships often define them. Those who are unable to overcome the trials placed before them often become crippled by these obstacles. They become stuck in a regressive loop, forced to endure similar tests and trials that are meant to strengthen their resolve, but instead, leave them in ruins. Such is the story of the one young girl who was sexually abused repeatedly when she was only nine years old. Research suggests that a traumatizing event of that magnitude can cause some people to develop dissociative identity disorder, experience PTSD or social anxiety, or find it difficult to develop healthy relationships. All of these are reasonable responses to a life event of this magnitude. Many people, men and women alike, are never able to fully heal and move forward after such trauma. That singular moment in life plays repeatedly in their heads and slows their actions.

Yet there are others, like TV star Oprah Winfrey, who rose from the ashes of her life—sexually abused by her cousin, raised in abject poverty, with all of the odds stacked against her. I imagine overcoming these things was not easy for her, but she did the work and forged ahead, forever sketching her name in the universe.

I'll admit, I have to periodically remind myself that there are no mistakes in life, only lessons. There is no right or wrong choice and no good or bad path. Only choices

that lead to the lessons you need to learn at that time
and space in your life. Once you learn the
lessons you'll stop making the choice.
—CANDRAADIASOUL CONNECTED

The example provided may seem like low-hanging fruit because so many people had to endure and their stories were never told. However, it is used to serve the purpose of how the most disgusting event happppened in Oprah's life taught her a lesson that could be applied in every aspect of life in order to fortify her purpose. I once heard Oprah say in an interview that the way she managed to maintain her wealth was because she physically signed every check. This habit could be attributed to an amazing work ethic, or she could have also learned at an impressionable age never to trust anyone fully, despite their best intentions.

The same can be true in a variety of situations, where someone could have accepted the seemingly "bad hand" that they were dealt in life and given up completely. I could use Jennifer Hudson, for example, who managed to land a secure place on the biggest television show in the world, at the time, *American Idol,* broadcasting its views to an audience of upward of 60 million people at times. She made it to the top three in one of the hardest vocal competitions during one of the hardest seasons. She was not only a contender, but she could have won if not for a tornado that blew down hundreds of landlines in Chicago, where her primary fanbase was unable to call in to vote. She was dealt a devastating blow. She was kicked off the show, and Fantasia Barrino went on to win. She could have easily gone the way of the countless people who auditioned for *American Idol* and didn't win (this author included, lol*). Instead, Jennifer Hudson rolled up her sleeves and auditioned for *Dream Girls* to star alongside Beyonce. Rather than allow the thought of all of her failures to consume her, she boldly took control of her role as Effie White—and the rest is history. A dimly lit star went on to become one of the biggest stars in Hollywood, earning the distinguished title of EGOT, an acronym describing someone who has won all four of America's top performing arts awards: an Emmy (for television), a Grammy (for musical recordings), an Oscar (for film acting), and a Tony (for theater acting) award. "EGOT" is a title that very few people in the entertainment industry can claim.

These are two extreme examples of following your dream until the conclusion of the story. So many people start the process and give up midway because things never seem to work out, failing to realize that in any great story arc, the hero is challenged in a way that would make many people give up. But the hero's resiliency forces him or her to overcome obstacles and eventually fulfill their purpose. As the Bible tells us, "*The race is not given to the swift, nor to the strong, but to the one who endureth until the end*" (Ecclesiastes 9:11).

THE JOURNEY OF SELF-DISCOVERY

"To begin to think with purpose is to enter the ranks
of those strong ones who only recognize failure as
one of the pathways to attainment."

—James Allen

18

Where are you on your journey? Is this where your story begins? Are you at the beginning, in the middle, or toward the end? As a clinician, I believe that awareness is the first step toward progress. You should strive to be intimately aware of who you are, where you are, what you have, what you want, and where you're going. Identifying these things will help to guide you on the journey to your purpose. If you are unaware and don't know how to start the process, there *are* a few manageable ways to get going. As the quotation above reminds us, you just have to begin to think.

ESSENTIAL QUESTIONS

Start by answering the following essential questions:

Who am I: _____

Where am I in life? _____

What do I have? _____

What do I need? _____

What do I want? _____

Where do I see myself going? _____

Where do I want to be? _____

Many people are often deterred from their dreams because they believe thinking about the "unimaginable" is a waste of time or the thought is scary. However, it's our mindset that determines our outcome. Thinking is a step, but writing down our thoughts can become a goal, setting reasonable action items becomes a plan, and following through can lead to purpose. Magical thinking is a coping mechanism that kids often display. They believe in Santa or the Easter Bunny and can accept that their gifts come from some magical source. Parents, however, know the truth about the long hours of working, shopping, and wrapping said gifts so that the child can be pleased with what they discover. It is critical that we dream, but imperative that we work to make our dreams come true.

Although psychological therapy is often underutilized, it can be a powerful tool to help declutter the mind and explore the depths of one's purpose. If you are unaware of the obstacles that hinder you from being able to have agency, how can you operate in your purpose? Everyone needs to take accountability for their thoughts because, for the majority of us, that is the one thing that remains in our control. Self-development and introspection are critical to outcomes in life. When we believe we are happy, we find that we often are. If you believe you are depressed, you will only discover sadness. If you believe you have no purpose, then you will never be able to discover it for yourself.

In my work, I have become increasingly aware that much of the distress my clients endure is often because, at some point along their life journey, they have become disconnected from their purpose. They experience crippling anxiety because they fear facing the world, depression due to not feeling useful or needed, uncertainty about themselves because they move without direction, and isolation because they witness others seemingly moving along a path that they are unable to see clearly. Every subsequent session is centered around why they feel so disconnected and the pitfalls they experience.

I often ask my clients, "Do you know your purpose?" All of them seem to be initially perplexed by the question because they seek out therapy in the hopes that talking about their problems should be sufficient to work through their distress. They reveal to me that they have become stagnant and disheartened in life, contemplating the meaning and processing what appears to be their existential crisis at hand. They are seeking answers to what I can see clearly: they have not identified their purpose; worse yet, they have but have failed to act. When the initial shock of the question subsides, they understand why I asked the question and how it applies to their lives.

Awareness alone is not enough to quell the ache that resides in the depths of their soul. The universe requires us to act! Much in the same respect as I put pen to paper, awareness is meaningless without action. We often talk to ourselves in circles about the things that we want to do. We have an overwhelming desire to go on vacation but neglect to identify a destination, research the cost, book a flight, or reserve a room. We do not do the work required to achieve our desired goal. And all the while, we envy those who constantly post trips on social media, and we stew in the regret of not doing the work. Our feelings are only exacerbated by seeing those friends live their best lives. We want what they have, but we are not doing the work necessary to achieve our desired outcome.

Our purpose is much like this vacation: Everyone wants to go, but few actually make it happen. If you don't believe me, plan a trip. All trips start the same: everyone seems to be excited about going; they talk about it incessantly and flutter with glee basking in the fantasy of what it will be. After some time, the destination is identified, the dates have been set, and lodging accommodations have been settled. Throughout the weeks, you find that the group of twenty people who were initially eager to go starts to slowly diminish as people remove themselves from the group chat or continue to engage, hoping to manifest this trip into being. Others meticulously plan, create a budget, adhere to it, and sacrifice to ensure they are not only able to go but maximize their experience. When the date comes, many find that their robust group of friends has turned into an intimate experience shared by only a few.

In this example, we assume that everyone begins the process with the same desire and the same information. They have all been provided with the same timeline, and everyone has agreed to what they believe to be reasonable for them to go. As achieving one's goals/purpose is analogous to life, we can't assume that everyone has equal financial means, work flexibility, or familial obligations, for example. We understand that there are often extenuating circumstances that may hinder everyone in the group from proceeding with the same ease. Yet, that's life. We all want to reach our destination, but the starting line is not equal for everyone. Some must endure hardships that others can only imagine—but as the saying goes, everyone must pay the price. It's those who overcome their obstacles who enjoy the reward the most. Those with limited means may work an extra shift, make accommodations for childcare, or agree to work a major holiday to ensure their time off is approved. They don't make excuses for their limitations because their desire outweighs their obstacles.

RUSHING OR UNDERDEVELOPED

Purpose is but a block of clay ready to be molded by the sculptor, as a lump of coal only has as much worth as the pressure applied to it. Essentially, we, along with our purpose, can be shaped and molded into a masterpiece or formed into diamonds. Those who have discovered their purpose realize that they have the ability to shape their lives by molding their purpose until it becomes a masterpiece worth sharing with the world. Purpose is the clay, and we are the coals. The pressure applied to our lives either causes us to crumble or allows us to become diamonds in the rough. How we mold our purpose is a one-of-kind design that only we have the blueprint for.

This section serves as a word of caution, however. We have the innate ability to tap into purpose, but woe to those who act with experience but without knowledge. This thing within us called purpose (that for many lies dormant) is the essence of why we are here. We are born to discover it, created to master it, and designed to perfect it. Those who tend to be successful understand finding a gold mine means nothing if they are not willing to dig deep. Some begin the work and never complete it because life, too often, gets in the way. They are often the most unfulfilled, miserable, and toxic kinds of people. Knowing that their journey has come to an end as a work of their own volition, they are likely to discourage others from pursuing their goals.

Think about it. Throughout your life you have had many conversations with people with great ideas, even truly amazing ideas. They talk about their plans, how this thing can change the world, and how they plan to make all of this money. They are excited; it sounds good to you, and you may even wish you had come up with the idea. You feel a bitter sting of envy because you know that they are onto something. Fast forward a few months or years . . . and nothing ever comes to fruition. Why do you think that is? The answer is simple: people are energized by ideas but often exhausted by the work it takes to make an idea happen.

Recently, a close friend of mine, whom I deeply admire and respect, told me that they are unhappy. When I asked why, they informed me that despite having a high-paying job that garners them respect and power, they are unfulfilled. They then reminisced about the work they did in the community and how it brought them peace and joy. The only problem is that sometimes the things that edify us don't pay the bills.

A PURPOSE WITHOUT A PLAN?

Purpose is innate. We are fully born and developed with the propensity to fulfill every facet of our divine gifts. The universe places us in a position to attain a goal, provides us with friends to support us on our journey, connects us with mentors to work through our problems, and provides us with resources to complete the task. When we discover this gift, which for some may reside dormant in the recesses of the soul, we must nurture it with every fabric of our being.

Some people may feel that because they are aware of their purpose, things should immediately become clear. They are often discouraged because the only feeling worse than not knowing your purpose is not knowing what to do with it. These are the people who are often bitter or depressed because they have a fundamental understanding of a phenomenon that requires more effort than simply being aware. Your spirit will inform you when you are most connected to purpose; you can feel it shiver through your spine, feel it like butterflies in your stomach, or have a feeling of euphoria. I recently watched the movie *Bohemian Rhapsody*, which chronicled the story of the beloved rock group Queen. What touched me the most about the story was a moment when the lead singer, Freddie Mercury, connected with his purpose. He proclaimed that he felt as though he was doing what he was born to do. That feeling is priceless. Some of you reading this book may be chasing that high, or some of you may simply wish to understand. It's the conversation you have with the universe about why you are here and an answered prayer.

The novel *The Alchemist* suggests that the universe puts us on a path that leads us closer and closer to our purpose. Along the journey, you will face hardships and experience success at different times. The hard times are overwhelming for some, and as a result, their journey comes to an abrupt end. Many people walk away because they lack the fortitude to see their journey through. Others experience a modicum level of success and become content with whatever success they achieve but fail to satisfy their ultimate goal. This is why it is imperative that when you hone in on your vision, you have a clear plan in mind. Grow to understand the shape of your purpose, what it looks like, feels like, smells like, and even tastes like. It is a tactile sensation that only you know how to interpret. When you feel it, acknowledge it and check in with yourself to ensure you are always walking on the same path.

The more you understand your purpose, the more you understand the depth and reach of your life's work. In this moment I encourage you to write out the vision for your purpose so that you are aware of how you want to operate in your gift. These thoughts are not intended to remain rigid but should remain as fluid as your dreams. Write them down and rewrite them, work on them, and make adjustments as necessary. Your written words are there as a reminder for you to never shortchange your dreams, goals, and aspirations.

VISION PLANNING

Begin by writing your plan. Remember that it doesn't have to be complete now.

_____

_____

_____

_____

_____

_____

_____

A PLAN WITHOUT A PURPOSE?

It's imperative that we do things with intention. The problem is that most people are quick to act on impulse, but they often find that they are disappointed in the results. I've had many discussions with people who express that they feel like a ship without a rudder, wandering, lost in the middle of nowhere. Their attempt to find direction leaves them exhausted, and they feel like they're drowning. This feeling is common for many of us at some point in our lives because life can make us feel as though we are lost in a sea of our problems with seemingly no way out. The encouragement is to move but to move with direction.

For example, if someone feels as though becoming a lawyer or doctor will help them feel closer to their purpose, one does not simply just apply to a program and hope to get in. They take the time to research the institution, the faculty, the staff, the student population, and the test scores required, etc. Then, they may consolidate the information and develop a plan. They start studying for the LSAT or GRE, order a test prep book . . . well, you get the picture. None of these things will guarantee that one will be accepted into the program or ensure success if and when admitted, but what they managed to do is develop a plan of action. The universe operates in conjunction with the actions that you take. If your plan is to go to school and you fail to take the necessary steps to get there, then you haven't done enough to inspire the universe, God, or the cosmos to operate in your favor.

If it is the case that you put in the work needed to find direction, the universe may further illuminate your path. Walking away from the light will only lead you into further darkness. Now, take that same example and do all the work. You may ultimately get accepted into the university, but discover a different passion along the journey that leads not necessarily to a university degree, but to your purpose. Your university time was merely a step in the right direction. No one gets to a destination without a place in mind. You will always find yourself perplexed that you ended up in Omaha when you expected to end up in New York. If you fail to take control of your destiny, then you are subject to end up wherever the winds may take you.

WRITING THE VISION

Growing up as a Christian, I attended church services regularly. One of the many scriptures etched into the recess of my mind is Habakkuk 2:2, which, in effect, states, "to *write your vision and make it plain.*" The importance of doing so is to better communicate your desires, not only to yourself but to your support systems. There are people in your corner who stand ready to support you at any given moment, but you must be clear about what it is you want them to support. This doesn't imply that you have all the answers; you are just able to help them help you navigate the roadmap to your success plan. For example, many people talk about writing a book, but we all often find that people listen halfheartedly. They grin and smile because it sounds good in theory, but anyone who has ever written a book understands that it's not as easy as simply saying you will do it.

When I defended my Ph.D. dissertation, my department dean, who was one of my committee members, told me that she stood ready to support me in anything that I chose to do. With a gleeful heart, I reached out to her sometime after the defense and informed her that I wanted to write this very book. She inquired about what I wanted to write about, what was the name of the book, how I intended to write it, what voice I wanted to use, who my audience would be, and if I had an editor in mind. I had the answers to some of these questions, but I realized I wasn't nearly as prepared as I thought. The dean reinforced her commitment to helping, but I was hesitant and unsure of myself. There aren't many times in life that someone tells you that they support you and actually mean it. Now that I had set my intentions, expressed them to others, and had a goal in mind, I wasn't sure I was even capable of achieving it!

What I experienced is one of the many tricks our minds play on us when we are in pursuit of our purpose. Doubt causes us to second-guess ourselves. Fear paralyzes us, and uncertainty creeps in when we think that no one will support our cause. What I've grown to realize, however, is that the journey is for me and me alone. If no one ever reads my work, I will still be able to rest assured that I completed a task that was in my heart, and furthermore, the fruits of that labor may not even produce until after my life is over. I have decided in my heart to start the journey; more importantly, I have committed myself to completing it.

With renewed self-assurance, I began to write down everything that came to mind when I thought about purpose. I would see posts on social media that inspired me, read books to reinforce my resolve, and even pulled from conversations I had with people in my life. It is imperative that we write down our vision so as not to forget what our goal is and what we hope to accomplish. I know from experience that the end result may not look anything like what you had in mind originally, but the act of writing things down helps you formulate a road map for future success. Even now, as I write, I cross out the mistakes or misplaced words or sentences because they may be useful elsewhere in this passage. My advisor encouraged me to write and keep writing, to edit and edit again. We are all amalgamations of our multiple successes and failures; the road becomes clearer as we continue to navigate through the field of our failures to a pasture full of success and accomplishments.

The art of writing is merely one road along the path. We write to make clear our desires, add as we go along, edit as needed, and accept things for what they are. As a psychotherapist, I often encourage my clients to journal as a means to process their inner thoughts and find clarity in their situation. Most people typically take that to mean that they should write down all of their negative thoughts, and they keep journals full of their heartbreaks and traumas. While this is completely appropriate, they are only half-doing the work; it is equally important to journal about the good as much as the bad things that happen. When clients start to regress or get hard on themselves, they tell me that they've journaled, and they question why they don't experience as much progress as they'd hoped. I then inquire if they are writing down all of the positive gains they have had—because our journey is more than the good or the bad, it's the totality of our lived experiences. I share this in the hopes that you write down everything! Sometimes our best ideas happen by mistake.

THE FLOW OF THE UNIVERSE

Our life force is intricately connected to the flow of the universe. When we are in alignment with the winds of purpose, this alignment propels us closer to our destination. While on the quest, it is important to check in with your energy. The people, places, and things that disrupt our energy can interrupt our purpose. They weigh us down with their negative life force, and we can be caught up trying to work through negative feelings instead of what we are destined to accomplish. If you find that your energy is interrupted and disturbed by the people you associate with, you may need to reconsider your circle. Proverbs 27:17 indicates that *as iron sharpens iron, so must we strengthen our brothers.* The people in your circle should pour into your life, uplift you, support you in doing right, and provide constructive criticism, not just their negative thoughts. Nothing interrupts your flow more than someone negative in your inner circle, whom you allow to weigh you down with pessimism.

While attempting to operate in purpose, you must learn to tap into your own flow. Find your rhythm, the environments that you work best in, the people who inspire you to work harder, and the relationships that support your growth. When you learn to work in your own flow, you will find that you will be able to accomplish more. There is a story in *The Alchemist* where Santiago is challenged to turn himself into the wind. What seemed like an insurmountable task became a reality when he learned to unburden himself of the doubts and fears of "what if."

The tools to accomplish these tasks have been provided in many forms in cultures and religious practices across the globe. Mediation is a great way to learn to release yourself from these weights, as are prayer, grounding, and healing circles, to name a few. When invasive and negative thoughts interrupt our peace and create distractions from moving forward, it is important to have a variety of tools to help you manage along the way.

INTENTIONALITY

On Solange's album, *A Seat at the Table*, she has an interlude titled "Do Nothing Without Intention." That loop has been stuck in my head for the last few months; it resonates with me deeply. What do you ultimately hope to accomplish? Why are you doing what you're doing? How much thought have you put into what you're doing? How hard are you working towards your goals?

We often say that we want things for ourselves and for our future, but many people stop after that thought. They believe that if they say it enough, it will happen—without a plan or without direction. I found that I have often fallen victim to this frame of thought. In 2019, for example, a few of my friends began planning a trip to Ghana for New Year's Eve. I continued to tell anyone who would listen that I would be in attendance. I did not save money, look up flights, check out the events on the website, or make any meaningful actions that would secure my trip. Suffice it to say that when the time came, I wasn't in attendance. In the past, I would say that I wanted to go somewhere, and I did something and it always worked out. This example taught me that I cannot plan haphazardly; I need not only to set my intentions, but I need to put the work behind what I hope to accomplish.

TAPPING IN

Purpose has no respect for the person. Don't allow personal insecurities to stop you from fulfilling your goals. As a doctoral candidate and Ph.D. recipient, I have been blessed to make purposeful connections; however, as a photographer, I have been placed in rooms with senators, millionaires, and others of significant influence. My purpose at those moments placed me in spaces that degrees and accolades could not.

When someone is tapped into their purpose, the universe seems to be in alignment. This is not to say that life doesn't happen to those who are tapped in. They are just the ones that vibrate on the same frequency as their intended purpose. Shonda Rhimes described this feeling in an interview with Oprah as a humming she feels when she is inspired. The impulse to tap into her gift and purpose is so strong that she can recognize the hum of the song when it's singing out to her.

Think about a time in your life when you were completely tapped in, when all cylinders were firing and you were able to execute said task as if it were second nature. What did that feel like? Did you hear a buzz, or feel euphoria, were you energetic, or did you feel a force propelling you in that direction? These are the signs that you should be aware of when you're in the moment. To recognize it is to be aware of what it feels like and what it requires to get that feeling again.

Things to Consider:

How mindful are you about your goals?

_____

Are you operating with intention?

_____

Are you connected to your vision? Or is it still underdeveloped?

_____

Do you have a plan? If so, how do you intend on manifesting it?

_____

CHAPTER 3

FALLACIES

The Greatest Lie Ever Told:
"I have no purpose, I exist in this space
and time to occupy space, go through
the motions, and eventually die."

Are we merely vapid, useless sacks of blood that God took nine months to create, ultimately to serve no purpose? Make that make sense! This lie is similar to anxiety—the irrational, extreme delusion that we are worthless and life truly has no meaning.

As a psychotherapist, I see many clients present with anxiety, depression, and stress because they fear that their life has no value; thus, they have no direction. In a session with one of my clients, he expressed that he felt as if he had reached the proverbial fork in the road. He described it as though he was looking at the many directions his life could take, and he was just waiting for a purpose to find him. To which I exclaimed, "All paths lead to purpose! You just have to start the journey!"

The journey to success begins with movement. Nothing in life is handed to us. We must fight and scratch and claw our way through the ebbs and flows of life. Our purpose is intended to provide direction, clarity, and a deeper connection to the creator. This isn't new information, but at times, we need subtle reminders that we must put the work behind our desires, and that includes operating, finding, and living with purpose.

A story I recall hearing when I was younger explained why the color black was not in the rainbow. As best as I can recall, the story goes like this:

One day, God called all of the colors together because he had a magnificent plan in mind. "Purple and Red," he exclaimed. "You will be placed on the ends of this masterpiece." "Blue and Orange," he proclaimed. "You will be here and there. Yeah, that looks great!" he exclaimed.

"Yellow and Indigo, you provide just the splash I need to make this right. Green, you are serene, and I need to place you in the middle.

There you go, My Beautiful Rainbow!"

At that point, Black was standing on the outside, wondering where he would be placed and excited at the possibility. White was starting to think the same as they eagerly awaited instructions. Sensing their anxiety, God turned to them and said, "I have another job for you."

Sad that they could not be a part of the rainbow, they listened attentively. "White, I want you to drape the sky to provide shade to my greatest creation, to hold water for life."

All the colors were given their assignments and were very pleased. But there stood Black, alone and without any instruction from God. Black looked up and asked in the innocent voice that only a child could speak, "I noticed that you draped White and Blue across the sky, and even Gray has its place. Yellow is the color of light, placed in the Heavens to shine bright. Orange has even kissed the Sun or Red when it's warm. Purple adorns the shoulders of kings, and Greens have all been placed in the Rainbow. What about me? Where do I go? Where do I belong? Where will I show?"

Then God, with a sweet and gentle smile, turned to Black and replied, "My child, I did not place you in the rainbow, or drape you across the sky, because I have cloaked you across the universe. You are the canvas on which I create my greatest work. I created light to illuminate your brilliance, and who better to allow you to glow than a Yellow? Black, you are the backdrop of my most magnificent creation; you frame every color perfectly. Alas, you cannot be in the rainbow because you outshine every color in creation."

This story reminds me of a universal human experience. We sometimes look at the progress that everyone else has made and minimize ourselves. Jealousy and envy become the enemies of purpose. When we attempt to measure ourselves against others, we begin to doubt ourselves and perpetuate the lie that our lives are without purpose. In this example, Black felt ostracized and questioned her place in the rainbow. If she had been included, then its larger purpose may not have been achieved. The color Black in this story was focused on comparing itself to the others, which served as a distraction from its true purpose.

THE LIE WE TELL OURSELVES

"When you stay on purpose and refuse to be discouraged by fear, you align with the infinite self, in which all possibilities exist."

—WAYNE DYER

Too often, we tell ourselves that we don't have a purpose; therefore, we fail to plan for the riches that the universe wants to provide for us. We are stopped dead in our tracks by our own fears and hesitation. We surround ourselves with people who do not have the imagination to see our dreams, so they weigh us down with their negative thoughts and project their insecurities into our lives. We find ourselves pouring our energies into our work, kids, and extracurricular activities to stay busy, and we are still left with the feeling of emptiness.

A part of the work that I do is challenging negative thoughts and dealing with cognitive distortions. In essence, the way that we perceive the world shapes the way that we approach any situation. In the book, *Mindset*, by Carol Dweck, she explores the concept of growth or a fixed mindset. When we see the world through a fixed mindset, we perceive that our situation is unchangeable and that we are powerless to affect change in our lives. When we have a growth mindset, we see the endless possibilities that are before us. Adversity cannot affect a growth mindset because we see a ladder when others see locked doors. The intention behind this section is to challenge you to be the "author of your fate and the caption of your soul," as described in a passage from the poem *Invictus* by William Ernest Henley.

As undergraduates, we were encouraged to learn this poem to teach us that no matter the circumstances, we are strong enough to endure. The path to purpose is not only waylaid by fear and doubt; there are also those among us who get sidetracked by the simple pleasures in life. We overindulge in things that provide satisfaction at the moment and become satiated by these things. There is nothing wrong with this; however, if your goal is to discover your purpose, you must learn to enjoy life but also to get back to the work. In *The Alchemist*, the story of the wise man beautifully illustrates this point:

> A certain shopkeeper sent his son to learn about the secret of happiness from the wisest man in the world. The lad wandered through the desert for forty days, and finally, he came upon a beautiful castle, high atop a mountain. It was there that the wise man lived.
>
> Rather than finding a saintly man, though, our hero, on entering the main room of the castle, saw a hive of activity. Tradesmen came and went, people were conversing in the corners, a small orchestra was playing soft music, and there was a table covered with platters of the most delicious food in that part of the world. The wise man

conversed with everyone, and the boy had to wait for two hours before it was his turn to be given the man's attention.

The wise man listened attentively to the boy's explanation of why he had come, but then told him that he didn't have time just then to explain the secret of happiness. He suggested that the boy look around the palace and return in two hours.

"Meanwhile, I want to ask you to do something," said the wise man, handing the boy a teaspoon that held two drops of oil. "As you wander around, carry this spoon with you without allowing the oil to spill."

The boy began climbing and descending the many stairways of the palace, keeping his eyes fixed on the spoon. After two hours, he returned to the room where the wise man was.

"Well," asked the wise man, "Did you see the Persian tapestries hanging in my dining hall? Did you see the garden that it took the master gardener ten years to create? Did you notice the beautiful parchments in my library?"

The boy was embarrassed and confessed that he had observed nothing. His only concern had been not to spill the oil that the wise man had entrusted to him.

"Then, go back and observe the marvels of my world," said the wise man. "You cannot trust a man if you don't know his house."

Relieved, the boy picked up the spoon and returned to his exploration of the palace, this time observing all of the works of art on the ceilings and the walls. He saw the *gardens, the mountains all around him, the beauty of the flowers, and the taste with which everything had been selected.*

Upon returning to the wise man, he relayed in detail everything he had seen.

"But where are the drops of oil I entrusted to you?" asked the wise man. Looking down at the spoon he held, the boy saw that the oil was gone.

"Well, there is only one piece of advice I can give you," said this wisest of wise men. "The secret of happiness is to see all the marvels of the world, and never to forget the drops of oil on the spoon."

THE LIE WE TELL OTHERS

Lie # 1: I have a plan. Growing up as a Christian, I often heard the phrase "faith without works is dead." As the adage goes, those who fail to plan, plan to fail. Many people discuss things they plan to do, but their words are ultimately fodder; they fall on deaf ears and never manifest into something tangible. Plans are intended to help us organize our thoughts, create a structure to organize thoughts, and create actions based on the plan. One memorable way to refer to this kind of planning is the "Seven Ps: Prior Proper Planning Prevents Piss-Poor Performance." In other words, it is important that we create a plan and try our best to follow through.

Plans change, and situations often cause us to adjust how we approach what we hope to accomplish—and that's OK! If the COVID-19 pandemic has taught us anything, it has taught us to adjust our expectations, timelines, and how to survive in dire circumstances. Some people planned travel, work events, or social engagements such as weddings—the list goes on and on—but collectively, we had to sit in our respective homes and wait out the pandemic. Major life events occurred, and sometimes, we could not honor these events in the way we had in mind; many of us missed out on opportunities that we planned for. Others took advantage of this time in ways that set them up for success. I am not a proponent of coming out of the pandemic with all these major accomplishments, as our focus was on survival; I merely hope to use it as an example of how we must learn to adjust our plans and still move toward our goals.

Lie # 2: I have it figured out. This is another lie we often tell ourselves, and it perpetuates a delusional mindset. If you had it all figured out, you would not be reading this book. Having a plan or a goal is one thing; planning is another; and "figuring it out" comes with the territory. We often don't have it figured out until we complete the task. Even still, there are many things that we can learn from our experiences, and if lessons are learned, we apply them moving forward. It's similar to the endless updates we get on our phones or devices, as tech companies constantly try to figure out how to make their product more effective. If you have it all figured out, then you don't need help.

Lie # 3: I don't need help. The truth of the matter is that at some point in life, we all need help. Knowing who to trust, who can provide the help we need, and who will be willing to help may be the questions and concerns you should focus on. In an interview, writer/producer Issa Rae was asked about networking. She answered that the problem is that we often try to network up when we should be fostering the relationships that we have and helping our friends grow and build from there. Many people find that they are disappointed when seeking help from people who are not on their level. Not every friend has the capacity to help us in the ways that we need. Conversely, people who are more established may not be willing to reach back and help. Nonetheless, the fact remains that we all need someone to help us and push us forward. My late grandfather would say, "If you're pushing someone up, you can't be far behind." Seek relationships with people who are moving forward with their life's plan, help them, and seek help from people who are motivated to watch you succeed.

It's equally important to understand the type of help you need. We tend to confuse conversations with help. The problem is that we get offended by criticism when talking about our plans, and we get upset because people don't truly understand our needs. When planning, identify your deficits, where you could use some help, and what that means for you. When you can clearly articulate your needs, you are more likely to receive the help and support you desire.

THE LIE WE TELL THE UNIVERSE

We often tell God, the Universe, the Creator, Mother Earth, or whatever you wish to call her, that we are not special. We have no purpose; we are useless and serve no purpose whatsoever. At various times in life, we may feel as though this is the absolute truth—until we stumble onto our reason for being. When we make these declarations, we are telling the essence of our true self that we are not important and only taking up space. When these cognitive distortions enter our minds, we need to reset and do some mindfulness training and cognitive reframing.

Today, I listened to a sermon about 12 chords inspired by a documentary about the rock music producer Quincy Jones. One of the influences in his life, the famed French music teacher and conductor Nadia Boulanger, encouraged him in 1957 to strive to reach his full potential with the twelve notes on the musical scale.

"Quincy, there are only twelve notes," she said. "Until God gives us thirteen, I want you to know what everybody did with those twelve. Bach, Beethoven, Bo Diddley, everybody—it's the same twelve notes. Isn't it amazing? That's all we have, and it's up to each of us to create our own unique sound through a combination of rhythm, harmony, and melody."

Boulanger pointed out that every musician who ever lived composed their greatest works with the twelve notes we are all given. What will you do with yours? To put it another way, evoking another American musical icon, we all have the same 24 hours of the day as Beyoncé.

- What will you do with your time?
- What will you make of yourself?
- How will you live up to the life and the gifts that have been bestowed upon you?

We are all essentially working with the same elements. We can create magic when we realize that everyone who has ever made or created anything did so with the use of the same tools that we, ourselves, have.

COMPARISONS

"Comparison is to look beyond your own plan,
to see the plan of others."

—Yasmin Mogahed

My late grandfather was the leader of a musical group called The Mighty Gospel Revelators. There was something so special about his voice that when he sang, you couldn't help but feel chills down your spine. The members of this quartet sang together for over 40 years. They had a special bond and blended together perfectly. I recall my grandfather telling the story of how one of the members started to compare himself to my grandfather.

One night in concert, this individual took it upon himself to try to hit a note that only my grandfather could execute. Suffice it to say, it didn't go over well, and the guy never tried it again. In this example, said member started to compare his gift to that of my grandfather and attempted to walk a path he didn't belong on.

When we compare our gift, purpose, or life to others, we start to focus on what they are doing and ignore the thing that makes us special. Furthermore, it halts our own progress because we stop what we're doing to look with envy at the actions of others. However, there is a notable difference between admiring someone and being inspired by their actions to aspire to achieve and model yourself after people who motivate you. When we compare ourselves to others, it only serves one of two purposes: to allow us to look upon others with envy or to look down on those who may not appear to be as successful. One creates seeds of doubt, while the other bolsters the ego. Neither of these results helps you toward fulfilling or finding your purpose.

SURVIVING THE PRESSURES OF LIFE

Many of us feel that we are burdened by the pressure to do, say, or become what others want us to be. But conforming to others' expectations provides a false sense of security and confuses our purpose. When you are unsure of yourself and what you are destined to do, you begin to operate in a space that fulfills others' needs and their purpose for your life. It becomes increasingly difficult when people we love are well-intentioned because it makes us want to make them proud, but this outside distraction takes us away from the reason we were meant to be.

I remember that when I was four years old, I saw a commercial for the famous Christmas-themed ballet, *The Nutcracker*, on television. I turned to my mom and told her that I wanted to grow up to be a ballerina. This expression became the source of many jokes about me in my family, and I am still somewhat embarrassed until this very day to confess this story. I recall my mother immediately looking at me and telling me "No, you want to be a lawyer." I instantly felt a sense of shame for expressing myself, and as I grew up, I acquiesced to her desires. Throughout my life, I just knew I was going to grow up to be an attorney, and I would say as much as I matriculated through school until I was accepted into college and the time came to declare my major. In that moment, I felt in my heart that I did not want to follow a path that I wasn't sure was my own; instead, I decided to major in psychology, which eventually led me to the path I am currently walking.

In this example, knowing that I was a Black boy growing up in a community that may not be accepting of a boy wanting to dance, my mother immediately attempted to correct my path. She anticipated the difficulties this desire might cause me, and she wanted to put me on a path more aligned with traditional gender roles. She said what she said out of love and concern, but at times, I can't help but wonder what my life would have been like if I had been allowed to dance.

I had to learn to navigate my life in a way that would make my family and community proud, in a way that was socially acceptable. I learned to suppress my true desires to appease those around me who seemingly wanted the best for me. If we are to survive life, we have to be headstrong in believing in ourselves and our own purpose. Who we are to become and what we are purposed to do is an intimate experience shared between us and the universe. No one else can tell you what your path is, although they can influence which road you choose to take. We are all destined to arrive at our purpose, but the level of difficulty increases based on how we choose to move forward.

As I write this, the rapper/singer Lil Nas X comes to mind. He has paved a way for himself in the hip-hop community that sets him apart from his contemporaries. He has mastered the art of being himself, at least publicly, and he stands in his truth, even if he is perceived as a social pariah. I can only imagine the courage it takes to stand in his truth when it would be much easier to conform to socially acceptable standards.

Things to Consider:

What is distracting you or keeping you from your goals?

_____

Are you being honest with yourself and others?

_____

Are you comparing yourself to others?

_____

Is the pressure overwhelming?

_____

Have you been giving yourself a fair chance?

_____

CHAPTER 4

FEAR

"I've learned that fear limits you and your vision. It serves as blinders to what may be just a few steps down the road for you. The journey is valuable, but believing in your talents, your abilities, and your self-worth can empower you to walk down an even brighter path. Transforming fear into freedom—how great is that?"

—SOLEDAD O'BRIEN

In 2005, Samuel Jackson starred in the critically acclaimed movie *Coach Carter*. Throughout the film, he chided his students by asking them, "What is your deepest fear?" I, like the students in the movie and much of the audience, had no idea what his intentions were for asking such a simple question. It wasn't revealed until a pivotal moment in the movie where the poem by Marianne Williamson was quoted. "Our deepest fear is not that we are inadequate. Our deepest fear is that we are powerful beyond measure..."

The essence of greatness is revealed by those who overcome the hardest obstacles, not because they are naturally endowed with the ability to achieve but because they fight through their anxieties. It reminds me of one of my favorite anime, *Naruto*. Naruto Uzumaki is the protagonist who came from humble beginnings and made great strides in his development. But it's not Naruto's tale that I want to discuss. It's an episode when Choji, the overweight, underdeveloped, less talented character, is challenged to step up. Even though we all knew death was imminent when he rose to the occasion, it sent chills throughout my body. He fundamentally understood that the challenge before him was something he was uniquely qualified for, and he didn't allow fear to stop him. Fear can be crippling and debilitating, and the reason why so many of us fail to even try: we are terrified of failing or frightened by success.

SHAME & FEAR: "I'M NOT GOOD ENOUGH"

As mentioned previously, *Coach Carter* (Samuel L. Jackson) cited a poem that suggested that our greatest fears are that we are powerful beyond measure. Some people have gifts that will elevate them beyond the stratosphere, but they fight with demons that keep them grounded. As the old adage goes, the bigger they are, the harder they fall. We live in an age of "cancel culture" that villainizes people for past mistakes, allows no room for growth, and is relentlessly unforgiving. The fear that is rooted in shame can be crippling and cause people to remain in a continuous loop of guilt that causes them to keep their distance and fly under the radar.

Limiting one's life can become a way of creating a proverbial hell loop, causing people to be tortured by their own guilt. Although every one of us has had to fight different demons at some point in our lives, the key to growth is learning to forgive ourselves, make amends as best as possible, and learn from our past mistakes. The fear of not being good enough or not deserving good things deprives the world of our gifts and purpose. However, it is important to remember that according to the scripture, "*Neither height nor depth, nor any other creature, shall be able to separate us from the love of God which is in Christ Jesus our Lord*" (Romans 8:39).

It's imperative that we keep in mind that no matter what we've done, we are able to find forgiveness. This is not an absolution for our past deeds, but rather an alternative for continuing to live a full life. Forgiving ourselves is not easy. I deal with a lot of clients who suffer from unimaginable feelings of guilt and shame. They must learn to reconcile with their past and make amends. For example, recovering addicts are challenged to reach out to those they have hurt in the past as a part of their recovery. Many people are unable to forgive, but offering a sincere apology along with changed actions is a start. Hopefully, finding peace with oneself will allow them to break the chains of shame that oppress them.

If this scenario applies to you, you must keep in mind that even if you reconcile the guilt of your past, your past may still resurface. In the event that it does, you can rest assured that you have done everything in your power to make things right. The hurt and pain may resurface, but you will no longer be prisoner to the ties that bind. Depriving the world of your gifts because you feel guilty does not only punish you. It is a punishment for the people who may be impacted by your purpose. Everything that we experience is a part of our journey, and we have to embrace every facet of our lived experience.

STEPPING INTO THE UNKNOWN

The path to our destiny is, at times, dimly lit. We are unable to see the forest through the trees and may find ourselves stumbling through the pitfalls of uncertainty. This can be a terrifying experience, causing many people to stop in their tracks and retreat to the light of being safe. In essence, when things become unclear, people resort to the things that they know, which provides a false sense of safety. Others become paralyzed and stop themselves in their tracks; they sit and wait to be rescued or allow their dreams to die in the dark pit of uncertainty and insecurity.

The fear of taking the road less traveled causes them to keep their lives small to avoid the greatness within. It is easier to avoid unwanted attention in the darkness. Some people have been conditioned to humble themselves to the point where they keep themselves small and unnoticeable. They may not suffer from the guilt of their past, but rather, they have told themselves that they are not important, not good enough, smart enough, or talented enough to step out of the shadows.

The late Dr. Martin Luther King, Jr. once said, "Darkness cannot drive out darkness, only light can do that. Hate cannot drive out hate, only love can do that." We were taught a very simple song at a very young age that essentially gave us the tools to pave the way for us to walk in our purpose. The song says, "This little light of mine, I'm going to let it shine." When we walk the sometimes dreary and morose road toward our purpose, we must look within for the light. Although the expectation is for light to come from an external force, sometimes we have to allow the light to emanate from within, even if it only provides enough light for us to see one step ahead.

Keep in mind that it is easy for us to be consumed by darkness such as insecurity, guilt, shame, and feeling insignificant. Negativity can spread like cancer, and light can seem to move at a snail's pace. An excerpt from the late Donda West informs us that "even if we are not ready for the day, it cannot always be night." In addition, there are a plethora of songs, myths, and stories that remind us that night or darkness is only temporary. So, when you find that you are in a dark place, just know that there is a light within that can drive away the darkness until the light of morning breaks through.

ALLOWING YOURSELF TO BE VULNERABLE

Life is ultimately a freefall: you can either enjoy the thrill of suspense or writhe in terror, anticipating the fall or expecting to fall flat on your face. The fear of failure is crippling to so many people that they chose not to act rather than experience failure. I cannot promise anyone who comes across this book that you won't experience pitfalls in your journey. I can only assure you that, as the famous ice hockey star Wayne Gretzky pointed out, "You miss 100% of the shots you don't take."

I could likely spend the rest of this book providing examples of the many people who have become successful in their purpose but who have experienced epic failures that cost them everything. But you can Google-search the story of anyone who has ever achieved a notable level of success, and they will all inform you that life ain't been no crystal chair. The poem "If" by Rudyard Kipling puts it this way:

> If you can make one heap of all your winning
> And risk it on one turn of pitch-and-toss,
> And lose, and start again at your beginnings
> And never breathe a word about your loss . . .

Kipling concludes that this is essentially the key to becoming a man. I, on the other hand, would liken it to you being able to find your purpose. Purpose is not measured by global or financial success, although the pursuit can cause some to risk everything that they have to obtain it. It takes a level of vulnerability to trust yourself with the light that has been placed inside of you and to develop the fortitude to pursue it.

Vulnerability requires wisdom: the wisdom to know who you can trust and how much information they can be trusted with. We must protect our light, gifts, and purpose, and it is not for everyone to understand. Many dreams have died because people decided to be vulnerable but trusted the wrong people with their ideas. People become insecure when they don't receive the support they desire from the people close to them; they allow others' lack of enthusiasm to cause dreams to wither and die.

The reality is that it is very difficult for some people who are too close to you to see your vision. That is because they often have a version of you that they created for themselves. This is why therapists cannot see friends or family in their private practice. It is very difficult to remain objective when we have already formed our thoughts and perceptions of the people close to us. For example, some of these people can hold our dreams hostage with the secrets they know about us. They have witnessed our failures, insecurities, and inability, and have seen us at our worst. They essentially reflect a light that brings out the shadows of our insecurities.

When learning to identify who you can be vulnerable with, you will be able to add lamp poles on your road to destiny. These are the people who believe in you, check up on you, hold you accountable, and provide constructive criticism. One must also know the difference between criticism and constructive feedback. These lamp poles help us to clearly define and refine the lump of clay that we identify as purpose. When writing this book, I asked my best friend, Mike Ortiz, to help me edit and provide feedback. I could trust him with my insecurities about writing and this thought of writing about purpose. What he provided was unconditional love and support, despite my grammatical errors and lack of direction. Conversely, I have told others that I'm working on a book, and like everyone who talks about writing a book, I was met with rolling eyes and condescending comments about people who never finish writing.

I had to learn whom to trust my thoughts with. Not everyone has the vision to see your ideas clearly. It has been said that we are the sum total of the people that we associate with the most. If you are surrounded by naysayers and haters, it is not likely that you will accomplish much. Energy is transferable, and it is easy to become dismayed by negative thoughts and people.

THE PATH OF DEAD ENDS

Some paths lead us away from purpose, people, and places, and become a maze in which we get lost because we refuse to see that there is no way out. Many people choose to go down the path that others have paved for them with no clear connection to what they are doing. In some cases, they can find that they are successful, but their purpose is never fulfilled. This is why we cannot conflate financial success or business success with purpose. There are many people with a lot of money who are left with a feeling of insatiable emptiness because they are only focused on the money.

The irony of this section is not lost on me. I have said time and again throughout this text that all paths lead to purpose, but it has to be stated that some people are on paths that don't belong to them or that they have no business being on. When you start the path to YOUR purpose, the steps that you take will lead you where you need to end up. When we are met with dead ends, we sometimes have to take a moment to reflect and re-calibrate in order to get back on track. By doing some introspective work, we may be able to identify whether the choices we are making are driven by purpose or by something else. If you find that a choice is not in alignment with your purpose, you may want to reconsider the road you are taking.

THE OTHER SIDE OF FEAR

It has been said that everything that we want is on the other side of fear. When we are able to conquer our fears, we are able to see the light more clearly. We realize that fear is an illusion keeping us away from accomplishing the assignment that is our ultimate birthright. This step was designed by the universe because it requires a sacrifice to ensure that you can be trusted with the gift that you have been given. This may seem like existential mumbo-jumbo, but any great text will confirm that what I am saying is true. This is the hero's journey: They are given a great task that is seemingly insurmountable, face trials that bring them to the brink of destruction, overcome adversity, and finally, they learn that everything they have endured and overcome has made the journey worthwhile.

If you have come across this book, it means that you are already on the right path. You are desperately searching to find the meaning beyond your existence, and you have identified a nagging feeling that needs to be nurtured and attended to. The journey for some will be long and arduous, but the pitfalls will only make your story more potent. Some people will get tired along the way and allow their fatigue to cause them to stop moving; others will forge ahead and quit when they are met with resistance; some will continue to press forward and become overtaken by fear; and some will see the journey through until the end.

Things to consider:

What has been holding you back?

_____

What are you afraid of?

_____

What are you willing to sacrifice to accomplish your goals?

_____

CHAPTER 5

IN THE HERE AND NOW

"The person without a purpose is like
a ship without a rudder."

—Thomas Carlyle

In psychology, Gestalt therapy places emphasis on gaining awareness of the present moment and the present context. The fundamental tenants of this person-centered therapy, according to its creator, the German-born psychiatrist and therapist Fritz Perls, can be summed up as follows: "The focus on the here and now does not negate or reduce past events or future possibilities; in fact, the past is intricately linked to one's present experience."

For those of you who are committed to pursuing your purpose, the first step is to orient yourself to the present. So many people fall into the trap on both sides of the road we are traveling, which is either living in the past or being so future-oriented that they are removed from the present.

Awareness is one of the key components to achieving any change in life. You should be aware of your past to avoid making the same mistake in the future and avoid living in the future, as it does not allow you to see the things that are happening in the here and now. As we discuss this journey of purpose, the thought of being "there" can be so seductive that we become lost in a fantasy of something we may never obtain. This fantasy blinds us to the reality of our situation and makes achieving the goal that much more difficult.

A part of the process is experiencing the journey. Without the journey, you will not have a story to tell to inspire others. Without this crucial element, your success lacks the gravitas to your story. By anchoring yourself to the present, you become hypervigilant in the pursuit of your purpose. When you are able to see the road clearly, you can make plans for the future. It's just important not to live in a place where you haven't paid rent. If you are unable to find the glimmer of purpose in your present, you risk mortgaging your future.

AWAKENED BY EXPERIENCE

Our past and future play a crucial role in who we are to become; one tells the story of what we have overcome, while the other is where we hope to go. However, it is learning from the experience that awakens the thing that lies within us. When we identify the role our experience has on the impact of our story, we can gain more clarity about our purpose.

PURPOSE PAINS

I am not a woman, but I, like every man and those who have not given birth or desired to do so, can all relate to the analogy of childbirth. Purpose is something that grows inside us, and as we nurture it, it becomes realized; we carry it within the depths of our souls, and everything that we do to bring it to fruition causes it to swell up inside us until it's ready to be released for the world to gaze upon its beauty. It is something that we birth from within, and we must all endure the labor pains that are associated with manifesting a living entity with us.

Some purposes are birthed in grief. Although this is not an ideal way of finding purpose, it has become realized by those who have experienced it. Countless names cross my mind as I think about the best example to illustrate my point. I think about Samaria Rice, a mother who lost her child at an early age in the most unfortunate circumstance. On November 22, 2014, Samaria's son, Tamir E. Rice, a 12-year-old African American boy, was killed by a police officer in Cleveland, Ohio, while he was carrying a replica toy gun in a park near his home. His story became national news and sparked protests around the world.

In the midst and through the chaos, hurt, and confusion, Samaria Rice became the face and the voice of a movement. She not only had to endure the physical pain of childbirth but her purpose was also birthed through the pain of her child's untimely death. While I do not know how or where she gained the strength to find a voice through the pain she endured, she did. As a result of her pain and grief, she has been committed to activism, giving back, and rewriting the narrative for her son and others.

TRAPPED FOR A PURPOSE

This scenario is complicated and just as cumbersome as finding purpose through grief. There is a well-known story about Joseph, "The Dreamer," who was sold into slavery by his brothers. His story, as told by Yehuda Altein, goes like this:

> Joseph was born in the Mesopotamian town of Haran, to his parents Jacob and Rachel. At the age of sixteen, he left Haran, along with his family, and journeyed to the land of Canaan, eventually settling in Hebron.
>
> When Joseph was seventeen, tension with his brothers came to a head. One day, Jacob instructed Joseph to visit his brothers in Shechem, where they were tending their sheep. Seizing their chance, his brothers threw the unsuspecting Joseph into a pit. A short while later, they spotted an Arab caravan passing the scene, and the brothers sold Joseph to the traders. He was eventually taken to Egypt, where he was sold to Potiphar, one of King Pharaoh's ministers. From there, he was sent to prison.
>
> When the king's royal cupbearer and baker were imprisoned, Joseph successfully interpreted their dreams, correctly predicting that the cupbearer would be released and the baker would be hanged.
>
> Two years later, King Pharaoh himself envisioned two dreams, which none of his advisors were able to explain. Remembering the Hebrew youth from his prison days, the cupbearer suggested that Joseph be summoned. Joseph, then thirty, interpreted Pharaoh's dreams as being a

divine prediction for seven years of plenty, followed by seven years of famine. He advised Pharaoh to prepare by storing grain during the first seven years.

Impressed by Joseph's wisdom, Pharaoh appointed him as his viceroy, second only to the king himself, and tasked him with readying the nation for the years of famine.

Meanwhile, the effects of the famine were felt in nearby Canaan. Hearing that there was grain in Egypt, Joseph's brothers journeyed there to buy precious food from the viceroy, not realizing that he was their very own brother.

To sum up, Joseph was imprisoned and harassed and endured all manners of pain and humiliation. Yet, it was during his time of captivity when he was placed in a position that saved Egypt and his people. His road led him through captivity in order to discover his purpose.

Like Joseph, some of us have been trapped in positions in life that have caused a great deal of distress and discomfort. It is this experience that has held you captive. Some may think that there is no way out of the grips of despair. However, in time and with awareness, these experiences can activate your purpose. One example is the rapper Meek Mills, who spent a considerable amount of time incarcerated for mistakes made in his youth but who grew up to be an international star, turned prison reform activist to help other young men avoid the same experience and pitfalls.

Of course, all our stories won't be pretty and wrapped in a socially acceptable package. We must effectively play the cards that have been dealt. The key to our freedom is identifying why we have been placed in these prisons and how to find our purpose through captivity. These prisons are often not a physical place, but we have been confined to fear, anxiety, and feelings of self-doubt. It is the prison of learned helplessness and self-fulfilling prophecy, where we talk ourselves out of opportunities and into a mental confinement from which there is no release, because we are judge, jury, and warden. Until we can release ourselves from this prison through our innate abilities, we will be forced to serve a lifelong sentence with no hope of parole.

DIVINE PURPOSE

Some of us have been endowed with divine purpose, placing us in a moment where our unique gifts and talents are used to serve the greater good. I recall, in the summer of 2018, when Parisian resident Mamoudou Gassama climbed four stories up the outside of an apartment building to save a child's life. I imagine that morning, he had no idea that his day would end with him becoming an international hero, something that changed the course of his life forever.

While all purpose is divine, as it is given to us by the creator, some of us have callings that require us to be in places where only we can make a difference. Remain vigilant in the pursuit of your purpose; it just may be so divine that it changes the world. Purpose is the "sixth sense" given to us by the creator. It guides our pathway, leads us through danger, and gives meaning to the mundane things we do in life.

It is easy to tether ourselves in one direction or the other, holding on to the pain of the past or clinging to the future to escape the torment of being in the moment. We must learn to make peace with the present, and we must take the rainy days along with the sunshine. The present is all we will ever have, each moment being more precious than the next—both of which we can never get back. We can, however, shape our future by the choices we make day to day. We can stay stuck in our predicaments or make decisions to lead to a brighter outcome. Take the steps, and build your life brick by brick.

Create a checklist of the things you have done or need to do.

My Vision Checklist

1. _____

2. _____

3. _____

4. _____

5. _____

6. _____

CHAPTER 6

TIME

*"Time is basically an illusion, created by the mind to aid
in our sense of temporal presence in the vast ocean of
space. Without the neurons to create a virtual perception
of the past and the future based on all our experiences,
there is no actual existence of the past and the future.
All that there is, is the present."*

—ABHIJIT NASKAR

Some time ago, I watched a video of Jaden and Willow Smith talking about time being a concept. At the time, I didn't realize what they meant, because I had no real concept of time. I lived each moment as I was told, clocked in on someone else's clock; I made my decisions by the need that was most salient at the time. Now that I have grown and learned more about myself and the world, I realize that what the Smiths said was true. While we cannot control the clock, we have the power to take charge of every waking moment we have.

Time and purpose operate on the same universal scale. Some things require expedience and the powers that be to choose those who are ready to accept the call. Some things require patience, and so the purpose is not revealed until the appointed time for them to become realized. Either way, we must learn to master the art of timing. This is one of the fundamental principles of *The 48 Laws of Power* by Robert Greene. When we learn to master the art of timing, we are tapped into an elevated vibration of the universe. We can learn to manifest the things in our lives and learn that the effort that we put into our desires all come together in time.

PURPOSE REVEALED

Earlier, I mentioned the story of Joseph and how his ultimate purpose wasn't revealed until after the seven years of plenty, followed by seven years of drought and famine. Many of us must endure the pains of hunger to appreciate what it means to be full. We must suffer loss to respect abundance, and we must feel lost to understand what it means to be found. Many of you are reading this because your purpose has not yet made itself known. I encourage you to continue your journey with the confidence of knowing that it will become clear before the end of your journey.

PURPOSE DELAYED

We are the only ones who can control the outcome of our story. Every day, we make choices that either contribute to identifying our purpose or delay the process. Purpose is patient because, fundamentally, the universe understands who we are at the core. We are not smart enough to fool God into believing we do not have the potential to fulfill our destiny. We are only fooling ourselves.

My late grandfather would often preach the sermon of Jonah and the whale. Jonah was a rebellious prophet who decided that he knew better than God. He ran as far as he could, only to find himself in the belly of a whale. He would come to regret his decision as he had time to reflect on the choices he made. Ultimately, he came to discover that he couldn't run from his purpose; he could only delay it.

The same is true about each and every one of us. We have been endowed with free will and are responsible for our choices. However, we were sent here with a task, and it must be fulfilled. Our hearts cry out to us to complete our journey. We process it in our dreams, our spirits hunger for us to nourish it, and our minds remain preoccupied with the thought.

Some people have theorized that purpose is a living and breathing thing that desires to be fulfilled. Much like any living organism, it has to be tended to. We must pour love, light, water, and nutrients into it in order to sustain it. Even when we find ourselves walking in the wrong direction, we are able to give it life because we have heard the call. Sometimes, we walk the wrong path, but as long as we are walking, we provide the energy needed to give our purpose a pulse. Ignoring it all together will cause something inside of us to die. Regardless of how "successful" we are or how much money we have in the bank, it will never be enough to fill the void that is left in the wake of allowing purpose to die.

We have been given a task and a challenge to not be weary in our well-doing, for in due season, we shall reap if we faint not. Purpose can be delayed, but you will not be denied when you stay the course. Master what's in your control and wait patiently until the stars align. To some, this concept may seem hopeless and cause you to sink into despair, feeling powerless and hopeless. Others will read this and rejoice in knowing that all will be revealed in time. Our mindset makes all of the difference; if we continue to work and wait, we will all be walking in the bliss of fulfillment.

> *"The best way to lengthen out our days is to walk steadily and with a purpose."*
>
> —CHARLES DICKENS

PITFALLS

> *"You must first be who you really are, then do what you need to do, in order to have what you want."*
>
> —MARGARET YOUNG

Yesterday, after my ritual biweekly workout, I found myself lost in conversation with a friend talking about life. As we sat on the concrete stairs conveniently located adjacent to the gym, we somehow happened upon the topic of recreational drug use. He confessed to the litany of drugs he used prior to changing his life and described what he called "the crash."

One day, he found himself lost somewhere in the middle of South Africa and stumbled on a group of locals willing to show him the town. It led him on a journey that would prove to be life-changing in inexplicable ways. He explained that in his curiosity, he tried using a drug that took him on a high that removed him from the mundane minutiae of life and elevated him to somewhere beyond the stratosphere. The high he described was the most euphoric he had ever felt in his life. He found himself floating on a plane that had never been explored, and suddenly, life had new meaning.

The problem, he proclaimed, was not "the high." What scared him was the crash. As high as this magical drug had lifted him, the crash sent him tumbling to a depth that was lower than he had ever been in his life. It was at that moment that he understood the nature of addiction and the finality of life. He couldn't move, eat, sleep, or get out of bed. His body craved what he had been given just to feel normal. Yet, somehow, he managed to crawl out of the deep dark hole in which he found himself—and he never looked back.

What stands out to me in this story is that even a week after his high, he stated that his body still craved the drug. He felt his blood pulsate, and he quivered with excitement at the thought of reliving that experience.

Although the analogy is somewhat gratuitous, the parallel is undeniable. Discovering purpose is a high that extracts us from the masses of our ordinary existence. It causes our veins to pulsate and our hearts to quicken. We have found meaning in life and have touched the hands of God. Conversely, when we are suddenly dragged off of our perch, we find ourselves lost and bewildered when we become disconnected from the source.

It is how we handle the pitfalls that we experience in operating in our purpose that proverbially separates the wheat from the chaff. Purpose is the embodiment of a feeling telling us that we are going in the right direction. It is a vision with no sight and a feeling with no emotion. We sense what we can't fully see or explain. Many of us become frustrated because the high we experience has faded, and our sight has been obstructed by setbacks, rejection, failure, and disappointments. Based on the principles of the laws of attraction, the belief about purpose suggests that everything will work out in your favor if you are aligned with purpose. The complication in understanding this theory is that the path we take to fulfilling our life's mission includes these pitfalls.

The great poet Langston Hughes wrote the poem "Mother to Son," which, in the first stanza, portrays a mother explaining to her son that "life ain't been no crystal stair." This phrase counters the fact that many people have a "rose-colored glasses" vision of what walking on/in purpose looks like. That is because it is a rudimentary understanding of what we have been called to do. If you ask anyone who has ever worked hard to achieve anything, they will tell you that their success comes along with hardship. For every smile, there are a million tears; with every step forward, there is a stubbed toe; for every elevation, a broken bone; and for every success, a field of failures.

CHAPTER 7

MULTIPLE PURPOSES

"The mystery of human existence lies not in just staying alive, but in finding something to live for."

—FYODOR DOSTOEVSKY

This chapter is layered and may be a little more difficult to understand. Up until this point, I have defined and described purpose as one defining moment that completes us. In essence, it is and is not at the same time. Let me explain. Purpose is a living organism that resides within us, but it continues to grow and evolve along with our actions. We can accomplish parts of our purpose, but it will never be complete until our time on this plane of existence has expired.

Purpose is the embodiment of what it means to be alive. When we are born, we give our parents a purpose, and as we grow, we find ours. In that moment, a woman becomes a mother and a man a father. When that purpose is fulfilled, there still remains the entirety of everything that is within us. For a woman's job is not only to be a mother: she has dreams that extend beyond her ability to help bring life into the world. As children, our purpose in the moment may be to give our parents direction and to find ours along the path. It is the phoenix within us, born to die, to be reborn over and over again.

We all have multiple purposes. This is the fail-safe that the universe provides to ensure that the work is accomplished. Some people will simply never answer the call. Yet, there is far too much on the line to leave it in the hands of a single individual, although some people are called for a specific task that only they can accomplish. Free will is a gift and a curse, as it allows us all to make choices that are self-serving despite the anguish we might feel in the depths of our bowels when we ignore it altogether.

Those who act are the ones who find enlightenment and fulfillment, while others suffer in silence, never being able to find fulfillment in life. However, this theme is not the focus of this chapter. Rather, this chapter is dedicated to those who have fulfilled their mission and accomplished the goal of unlocking the door of mysticism and entering into the realm of purpose. Some discover that this is the end of the road, and they remain content with living in the bliss of crossing the threshold and discovering a singular purpose. They might remain there and feel at peace for their contribution to the collective. However, purpose is more nuanced than singularity. It is metamorphic and changes with the phases of our lives; it is sentient and self-replicating, with each replica having the ability to define its own meaning. When we are impregnated with purpose, the embryo takes on a life of its own.

Suffice it to say, our objective is to seek our purpose and continue to tap into ourselves until we have depleted our resources. We should leave this world having given everything we have, until the day we expire. The goal is to focus on each purpose, nurture it, develop it, perfect it, water it, and allow it to blossom.

OVERLAPPING PURPOSE

We must also remember that we should never assume that we are the only ones who have been given a gift, a thought, or a purpose. As previously stated, some purposes are time-sensitive, with little room for flexibility. When this is the case, purpose is implanted in multiple people at the same time. The person who answers the call reaps the reward. For example, as I write this, I recall a time when I was in my house, cold and shivering, and I found myself snuggling under a blanket, wishing I could maintain the feeling of warmth while being able to use my hands freely. A few months later, I saw a commercial for the Snuggly, and I couldn't help but feel a sting of regret for not acting on the thought. This is why it is imperative to act when we are inspired and recognize that there is a need for desires to be met.

We may also be called to complete multiple tasks concurrently. It is like being a student in any capacity. Sometimes, you have assignments due on the same day or take multiple exams in the same week. While it would be prudent to prioritize and organize to optimize success, the workload could be overwhelming, and the work still has to be done. Put another way, sometimes along the path, we have to complete missions and quests to unlock the key to get to the next level. The art of living is finding ways to make meaning of the time that we are given, which is not to suggest that we overwhelm ourselves with work and stay busy to avoid experiencing life's beauty. Rather, purpose is intended to keep pushing us toward elevating until we reach our final form.

CHAPTER 8

STEPPING INTO IT

"The greatest thing in this world is not so much where
we stand as in what direction we are moving."

—Johann Wolfgang Von Goethe

Time and again, I have reiterated that purpose is a journey, and we have to take meaningful steps in its pursuit to find it. Even when we misstep, we are still walking. Standing still gives us the same results. There is minimal danger when we stand in places where we feel comfortable, but our purpose begins to atrophy and die a silent death deep within us. If you are reading this book, then you have identified that you are in search of purpose, even if you have not been able to identify it. In the previous chapters, I have outlined some ways to start the journey. There is no road map to figuring it out, as it changes with each step you take. The main objective is to identify the need and to pursue it relentlessly.

While the pathway to the promised land is filled with mystery, one must still walk it, taking steps despite the pitfalls and obstacles that stand in the way. Eventually, you will step into it, even if by accident. It is because of your actions, work, and due diligence that you stumble across it. In these moments, it may seem like purpose occurs through happenstance. On the contrary, it was manifested through your actions. Through intentionality, we add straw to the motor that builds the stepping stones towards reaching our destination.

There is no right way to reach the end of the road. As J. Cole states in his song "Love Yours" in his 2014 *Forest Hill Drive* album, "The good news is you came a long way; the bad news is you went the wrong way." Sometimes, we may take the wrong path, but when we discover that we are walking in the wrong direction, it still adds value if we learn valuable information along the way. When we become aware that we are walking out of the way of our purpose and we course-correct, we can still salvage our purpose.

The universe sees that we are heading down a pathway that we do not belong on and attempts to nudge us in the right direction until we find our lane. If we are wise, we learn the lesson once so that we don't find ourselves walking adrift, lost in a sea of dismay because things "never seem to work out." Rather, we take what we have learned and use it to help us remain grounded in our aims.

STARTING OVER

Everyone can relate to the unbearable feeling of having to start over. It seems futile and difficult to accept that we have to start back at Square One. This may possibly be one of the most critical elements to finding and discovering our purpose. Having the ability to humble ourselves to start over may possibly lead us down a path that is greater than our wildest dreams. As I mentioned in the section about being on the wrong path, at times, we have to take backward steps to move forward. It may take you longer to get to your destination, according to the timetables you build in your mind, but you will arrive on time, even if it's at the last minute.

I have been seeing a lot of messages as of late that state something to the effect that it is impossible to be "behind" in life. When we are walking our own path at our own rate and pace, we will arrive at our purpose on time. We are not in control of the outcome of our actions; we are only responsible for acting. The universe does not operate with the same logic or principles as our humanity. The commandment we have been given is to seek, and ye shall find. We are merely responsible for one aspect of the directive.

STEPPING INTO GREATNESS

> *"The journey of a thousand miles begins with a step."*
> —LAO TZU

The road ahead is paved with different terrains, as Frost's poem "The Road Not Taken" illustrates. There are thorny patches, peaks, valleys, and adventures untold. You just have to start the journey. It is not always going to be an easy road to tread, and you have been given tools to help you along the way. William Shakespeare wrote, "Some are born great, some achieve greatness, and some have greatness thrust upon them." If you find yourself in any of these categories, you have come to the realization that there is a greatness inside of you that is inevitable. Despite your limitations, you can achieve greatness through your actions.

The first step you take tells the universe that you have accepted the calling. Every subsequent step says that you are committed to fulfilling it until completion. With each step you take in the right direction, you must strengthen your resolve, face your fears, overcome negative thoughts, and pursue your purpose relentlessly. For many of us, greatness will not be thrust upon us. We must fight for it with every fiber of our being. Greatness does not mean that your calling or purpose will propel you into a state of fame or acknowledgment. It may simply mean that you have completed the task that you were assigned. That is greatness personified, as not everyone will be fortunate enough to complete their calling with the clarity of knowing that they have fulfilled their purpose.

MEDITATION

I often encourage my clients to meditate to help them seek and find inner peace. It is a tool that most therapists and other healers recommend because it has been proven to be extremely beneficial. Even though I spent years telling clients to do it, I did not start to practice this in my own life immediately; when I did begin, I realized how truly amazing it is. Stress, anxiety, depression, doubt, and confusion live in our minds, and if we do not create a space to release these emotions, they will take up residence within our psyche. The practice of meditation allows you to release negative thoughts and gain clarity and inner peace. Why is this important to mention in a book about purpose, you might ask? Good question.

As you are on the path set before you, fear, doubt, worry, and anxiety will eventually find itself in your mind. It is natural to have some level of trepidation. It is one of our basic instincts to be leery about exploring new spaces and new things. However, you must not allow yourself to sit in these feelings too long. Sometimes, you need to do more than speak it. You must put things into action that will allow you to release those feelings. Meditation is an extremely helpful tool to accomplish this goal. As meditation is an art, it takes work to completely master it. I encourage you to start with 10 minutes a day of guided meditation until you're ready to do it for a longer time without assistance. If you don't take anything else from this book, please take this tool and implement it in your daily routine. You might find that you are generally less stressed, have less anxiety, and are not as consumed with the day-to-day problems in life that hold no meaning. With a clear head and a lighter heart, may your path toward your purpose be a peaceful one.

MINDFULNESS

Mindfulness is just that; being cognizant of the things you are doing, being present in the moment, and allowing yourself to think about who and where you are. Oftentimes, people get into a routine and just operate without being thoughtful of their actions. If your goal is to find and pursue your purpose, then you need to be hyper-vigilant and aware of what you're doing and why. For example, say that your purpose is to teach inner-city students to learn how to paint. You must be aware of your motives, why you believe your purpose is to help this particular community, and consider how your presence will impact them. Without awareness, we are acting on emotions that may not be secure or stable. If your purpose causes more harm than good, then you are on an ego trip that has nothing to do with anyone but you. If your goal is to make yourself feel better without consideration of how it may help or benefit others, then it's not your purpose; it's your ego.

> *"The goal is not simply for you to cross the finish line, but to see how many people you can inspire to run with you."*
>
> -SIMON SINEK

CHAPTER 9

IDENTIFICATION

"If you can tune into your purpose and really align with it, setting goals so that your vision is an expression of that purpose, then life flows much more easily."

—Jack Canfield

Purpose and success are not the same, no matter how hard we attempt to conflate the two. A person can have both, but they are not interchangeable terms, and the meanings may be subjective. They are not mutually exclusive, although they may overlap. They are both nuanced, and it all depends on how you define the two. Gifts and purpose can be in alignment, but having a gift may not be one's primary purpose. Those who find purpose find success, but people who find material or outward success may *not* find their purpose.

There are countless people who never achieve their goals, but it does not mean that they have no purpose. I think about my grandfather, a man who had a voice that would bring a tear to a man with a heart of stone. His gift was so incredible, but he never received the recognition he deserved in this life. After numerous attempts to break into the music industry to no avail, he decided to spend his days teaching and preaching. Although he never reached the heights where his musical talent could or should have taken him, he was still filled with purpose.

I can recall going to churches all my life and listening to him sing. I saw how the audience was filled with joy and tears as he serenaded the audience. He even met my grandmother while he was on the road singing with his group. (My dad was conceived as a result!) His gift was a conduit to his purpose, but singing professionally may not have been meant for him to do. I cannot speak to what his purpose was, but I can recognize that our purpose does not solely reside with our talents.

Conversely, when purpose and gifts are aligned, we find our divinity. The universe desires for us to live a life of abundance, operating in our gifts that bring us peace, and prosperity, and when we are able to do what we love, we live life at the optimal level. Despite my earlier sentiments, we must also recognize that there are those whose purposes are directly aligned with their natural gifts. We may never be able to quantify this claim, but I venture to guess that they are in the minority. To be clear, this is not a pessimistic outlook on gifts and purpose. I believe that any avenue to achieve our purpose is the correct course of action. I only hope to encourage people to look past their gifts when those gifts cannot bear fruit. The path towards achieving purpose is laden with pitfalls and traps. Many people have been lost in the maze of seeking celebrity, the quicksand of ignorance, and the trap of being singularly focused on one aspect of being. They become stuck knocking on the same door instead of finding new avenues of entry.

I recall having a conversation with my friend one day about his purpose. He quit his government job with a high-paying salary to start his own business. I was able to bear witness to the birth of his business and watched as he worked tirelessly on building his company. One day, I built up the courage to ask him what he felt like. He said to me that it felt like Christmas growing up poor. Each year has its own unique surprise, but the feeling is the same everywhere. You wake up with excitement after dreaming of Santa and can either find the toy of your dreams or a lump of coal. Nonetheless, it's still Christmas, and that joy follows you throughout the day. Sharing that even though every day isn't perfect, he is in love with what he does. He wakes up energized and excited to learn something new. His enthusiasm is infectious. He motivates everyone around him because, as he describes it, he has found his purpose.

PERFECTING PURPOSE

Now that you have discovered your purpose, what are you going to do with it? I believe that awareness is the first step towards progress, but if we don't do anything with that information then we are destined to fail. Purpose is not just something we must learn to recognize; it's something we must mold and shape to our will. We must constantly work on honing our skills. The more time we put in, the more skin we have in the game, and the more hours we put in, the better we become at identifying it, operating in it, using it, and helping others with it. It is an "iterative process," in the words of a dear friend. For some people, they recognize their strengths and play to them; others recognize their weaknesses and learn from them; then there are those who are aware of both and work on building themselves daily. What good is having a gift you never use?

When my university bestowed the honor of "doctor" on me, it thereby informed me that I have become an expert in my field to the highest level. This is certainly not to say that I have learned everything that I will ever need to know. It is merely to acknowledge that I have learned all that they can teach me. The real work begins after. There are no more homework deadlines and exams to study for. It is now my responsibility to read current articles and updates to the manuals. It requires lifelong dedication, requiring me to be knowledgeable and flexible. We must be willing to unlearn things in order to be relevant in the current climate. We must treat our purpose the same. We must be diligent in our pursuit and the same with perfecting our craft.

Things to consider:

How have you defined your success?

Do you consider success to be your purpose?

How much time have you put into perfecting your purpose?

CHAPTER 10

EXPLORATION

*"Everyone has been made for some particular work, and
the desire for that work has been put in every heart."*

—RUMI

WORKING

It is imperative that we are intentional about our purpose. It's not enough to say you want something. You need to pursue it with passion; work for it, work on it, seek it out, perfect it, nurture it, feed it, and water it in order for it to grow. In the Christian Bible, it tells us that *"Faith without works is dead."* You can believe that you are going to win the lottery all you want, but unless you buy a ticket, it will never happen. Everyone has to put in their 10,000 hours. There is no exception to this rule. If we are to find our purpose, we must master it. We have to be working toward it or working for it.

SEEK AND YE SHALL FIND

"Seek and ye shall find, if you build it, they will come, the journey to a thousand mile begins with a step. . . ." What do all of these sayings have in common? Let me help you: They all tell us that we are responsible for working towards finding it. It is not just a hope or a wish but rather an active pursuit. Some people might find what they seek on day one, but for others, it takes a lifetime. Ultimately, it's up to you to determine the timeline. How much work are you willing to put in to find what you seek? When running late for work or an important meeting, we will tear the house down looking for our keys. Why? Because time is of the essence. Go after your purpose like you do those keys. Turn over every pillow and check all the drawers. Look under the counter and check your pockets. It's bound to be somewhere, but it will not just pop up because you long for it.

CREATING A ROAD MAP

As a young man, I loved watching the *Harry Potter* series. As a grown man, I love them even more. There were so many lessons that one could learn watching those movies. For example, in one of the movies, Harry and the gang need to find something in Hogwarts, and they happen upon a map that shows the location of anyone in the building. This map was an essential element in the success of their mission. While seeking your purpose, you need to obtain a "magical map" that you store deep in your soul to help guide you along the path.

This analogy may seem somewhat convoluted, but I hope that you are able to look within as a guide to help you along your journey. We have been granted a gift called intuition, which can help us identify when there is danger or if we are safe. We learn to mistrust it because we often ignore it and misinterpret the feeling when we need it most. While we are along this path, our internal map can help guide us when we come in contact with people who hinder us or support us in our aims. Learn to recognize the feelings of safety and trust. You must first learn to trust yourself in order for your internal map to be effective. You must learn to feel safe with yourself because you can often do as much damage as others. We must learn our boundaries to know how far to push ourselves. We must also open our eyes to the people around us. How are they moving? And are they moving in a direction that we want to go?

PROXIMITY TO GREATNESS

While writing this section, I happened upon an article by David Burks, in which he argues, "You're not the average of the FIVE people you surround yourself with. It's way bigger than that. You're the average of all the people who surround you. So, take a look around and make sure you're in the right surroundings."

If you are seeking your purpose, you should surround yourself with people who have found it or are doing the same. It is also imperative that we assess, evaluate, and reevaluate the people in our sphere of influence. Take a good look at your friends, family, lovers, co-workers, and associates and determine if they inspire you to be great or if they enable your complacency. Being placed in circles of greatness can be daunting when you are not tapped into your purpose. Take hope that you are in the right room and that you deserve to be there. When you become aware that you are surrounded by greatness, know that there is room for you at that table. It's just up to you to take your seat.

It's equally important to determine if you have placed yourself in environments that do not challenge you, that don't align with your goals, or if you are in a place you don't want to be but go to out of habit or obligation. I am not saying to get rid of all of your friends and family. I'm merely suggesting that if this is not where you want to be, you should head in the direction you hope to be. It's a mindset and a way of life. If you surround yourself with positive people, you are far more likely to have a positive disposition. If you surround yourself with negative people, your outlook will likely be the same. I read a meme that said, "Notice your energy when you're around certain people. If exposure to them causes you to feel negative or positive, that might be a good place to start."

CONNECTIONS TO THE SOURCE

The universe will provide you with everything you need to fulfill your purpose. It will place you in circles of friends, colleagues, or whatever you need to help you get from A to Z. When you discover that you are on the path, the way will be made easy when walking in your light. The singer Erykah Badu did an interview on *The Breakfast Club*, television show, some years ago and talked about how the Jedi have a connection to the source. For those of you who know the story, you are aware that there are some Jedi who have a stronger connection and are thus able to use their powers more effectively. Similarly, we have all been endowed with a connection to the source. We are born with the innate ability to commune with the universe and ask for the tools we need to succeed.

When I was younger, I read the story of George Washington Carver, an African American scientist famously known for the creation of peanut butter. In the story, Mr. Carver was met with the dilemma of needing to discover a use for peanuts after encouraging farmers to plant this crop to replenish the soil for other crops. What stood out to me in the reading of this particular story was his prayer. His prayer was simple. He prayed that God would unlock the secret of the peanut.

While he is most known for peanut butter, he was actually able to discover over 300 uses for the now commonplace and extremely popular legume.

In this example, Carver displayed his connection to the source. While there are those who do not believe in a higher power, the universe, or any outside influence, the same is still true for you: there is a power inside of you that only you can tap into. You have experienced being at the peak of your abilities at least once in life, or you will. There is a mode that you can tap into that will bring out a side of you that you didn't know existed. We have all heard the story of the mother who lifted a car off her child. Digging into the depths of her inner strength, she mustered the courage to lift without thinking about how heavy the obstacle was in front of her. We are all able to do incredible things when we believe in ourselves. Find it!

CHAPTER 11

WHAT'S THE POINT?

"As you start to walk on the way, the way appears."

—Rumi

The discovery of purpose is a journey that we must all travel alone. It's in the moments of solitude that we hear the voice of the creator leading us down the path of least resistance, illuminating our path and guiding us without distraction. It is our innate desire for companionship that causes many of us to pick up drifters along the way. Carrying the weight of their distractions, we can cripple these drifters the further we pull them away from their north star, and they can slow us down to the point of stalling.

The Torah tells the allegory of Abraham and his covenant with God. In the story, Abraham was instructed to leave his family, his village, and his familiar surroundings to set out toward his purpose. He was instructed to go alone, taking only his wife, as she was in covenant with Abraham. God told him, He would give him every place where he set his foot, as He promised Moses. According to the text, Abraham, devoted in his faith, set out to leave but failed to follow the instructions as directed. He decided to take his nephew Lot. The story goes on to tell how in his desire to please God and himself, he created a series of problems that, according to many continue, to this day. While he was obedient to his God, he did not fully follow the instructions. He was ordered to go alone, taking only his wife, but instead, he took his nephew as well, and this action caused him to be taken somewhat off course. When he corrected his behavior, God gave him everything he promised in the covenant that they made—ultimately fulfilling his purpose, but with complications that could have otherwise been avoided.

In my humble opinion, with no intention of adding my own convoluted logic to this story, I believe that Abraham's actions are simply reflective of human nature. As mere mortals, we are subject to fear and distraction. When we take accomplices with us, we trust in the strength of our companions, believing that we can face obstacles with someone to help us fight whatever foes we may face. However, sometimes the company we keep causes us more problems and complications than going and doing things alone.

It is for this reason that we are all born alone. Yes, even twins have to exit the birth canal as individuals; as close as they are, they must make this journey to this plane apart. The universe has set a purpose for everyone; this infinite wisdom has designed for us to enter the world alone and return to its embrace in the same manner. Everyone has their own divine purpose, and it takes effort from every individual to accomplish these goals, even if it takes the right partnership for the objective to be met.

I can understand how you might be confused by this last statement. Let me clarify. Even when two or more people join forces to create something magnificent, each individual has to travel their own path to be in place in order to be in alignment. They must be born to their families, grow in their own communities, learn from their instructors, manage their hardships, and continue to pursue their goals. Their combined experiences bring them to a place where they can take their knowledge, gifts, and skills to bring a larger purpose to fruition.

THE PATH OF EXPECTATIONS

Many people feel as though they have been put on a path that they did not choose and that outside forces are pushing them toward an unavoidable end. They feel powerless and ushered along a road that they prefer not to be on. With my extensive television knowledge, I love to watch shows like *Game of Thrones*, where many of the characters claim to have a birthright to The Iron Throne. They were raised to believe that they were endowed with the right to rule over a kingdom. This role came with expectations of who they were, how they should behave, and what they deserved.

Better yet, we can consider the royal families in Europe. I imagine that the weight and pressure on Prince William to become the king by birthright has caused him to live a life that does not allow him to ever escape his destiny. He must adhere to rules, rituals, and expectations that do not fall on his younger brother, Prince Harry. Thus, Harry has been able to abdicate his position, while I imagine William can never free himself from the shackles of his inheritance. This is not to say that William does not love his life and that he does not desire the position. It just may be possible that he has never been able to dream of anything different.

In fact, some people may feel trapped by the expectations of their birthright, feeling as if they are bound by the limitations of their families' histories and expectations. This feeling is a trap that keeps people from branching out and doing things that make them uncomfortable but ultimately bring them joy. Our purpose does not respect our rituals. It causes me to think of the story of King David, who was not or should not have been considered to be king. He was not the oldest, the smartest, the best looking (I'm guessing), nor the most successful of his brothers. In the story, the prophet was instructed to anoint a new king. When he arrived at David's house, his father tried to present all of his other sons before he even considered David, the shepherd boy. The rest of the story is history, as we know that despite his birth order and what was expected to become of David, he became king and the apple of God's eye.

Understand that despite your circumstances, you have been endowed with a purpose that supersedes those circumstances. People born into abject poverty have acquired riches beyond measure, while those born with means cannot necessarily find peace or happiness. What is inside us comes with a wealth that cannot be measured, a light that cannot be contained, and a master key that unlocks padlocked doors that are not meant for us to enter. Fear keeps us from trying, from living, and allowing ourselves to make mistakes and try something new.

Living through a modern age of quarantine due to the COVID-19 pandemic has shifted the landscape of the world. We were forced to sit still, stay in place, and separate ourselves from the daily distractions of the world as we knew it. We may never be able to quantify the toll of the pandemic in lives lost, dreams deferred, long-term health complications, and much more. It is with great reverence that I mention the pandemic, as we were all impacted by the devastation we were plagued with. I, like many others, lost people who were dear to me, and I was unable to honor their lives by attending their funerals in person.

As it relates to purpose and the contents of this book, I want to highlight some of the material things that people have lost, as material loss is often the easiest to understand; however, I want to be very clear that I understand and respect that so many of us lost much more, and we are still dealing with the impact of these losses.

In material terms, however, the unprecedented, heretofore unimaginable socio-economic impact of worldwide pandemic-driven shutdowns seemingly halted some people's dreams in their tracks. The buildings they just acquired, the restaurants once scheduled to open, the homes they purchased to rent out—were all upended. Some lost everything they had with a sudden twist in fate. Many never recovered and gave into the despair of all that they lost, while others started thriving businesses, podcasts, YouTube channels, etc., and found a level of success that would have otherwise seemed impossible. Was it fate that brought them to this destination? Or was it alignment?

I believe that it's human nature to attribute our misfortunes to fate but our successes to our individual attributes—though the reality is usually somewhere in between. When we make steps toward our goals, the winds of fate and fortune are blowing at our backs, pushing us toward purpose, and easing the burden of the weight of the journey. Nothing happens without intention; we are all ultimately responsible for what we choose to do with our time. I laugh internally as I write these words because I have been working on this book for years, and while the words have welled up inside of me, I often found myself avoiding my computer, refusing to read or write, and expecting this message to be released into the world without working to complete it. If this book is ever to become a success, I know not. What I am painfully aware of is that it can and will never be if I don't complete it.

Many days, I have been waiting to be inspired to write. It is the hill that I have been willing to die on for years, as I talked about it in excitement with my friends, family, and even in job interviews. However, I knew in the depths of my soul that it could not happen if I didn't work at it. I said to myself and anyone who would listen that I only write when I'm inspired because I can tell the difference when I force myself to write versus when this overwhelming feeling overtakes my spirit and forces me to sit in front of this document. However, the reality was, and is, that until I became intentional about writing, I did not find the words. I wake up in fear that the universe will take this opportunity from my grasp due to my negligence because for a long time, I refused to put pen to paper for fear that no one would ever read my book. Rather, I fear they will judge me for not being a prolific writer, judge my grammar, dissect every word, and reject me as well as the message.

Fear is paralyzing, but it is an acceptable emotion to hide behind because we respond to fear in one or two ways: fight or flight. Running away has its virtues. We are able to survive the night, but the problems we face are often persistent. Jonah tried to run away from what he feared and hated, but he found himself at his destination anyway after an ordeal. I suppose his story wouldn't be significant had he done what he should have done without resistance—but there is no lesson in that. Purpose is not meant for our comfort. It is intended to heal the world. Purpose may emanate from within, but the light is meant to provide heat to those who are touched by it.

It reminds me of another story, this one from the Book of Matthew in the New Testament:

> "For it will be like a man going on a journey, who called his servants and entrusted to them his property. To one he gave five talents, to another two, to another one, to each according to his ability. Then, he went away. He who had received the five talents went at once and traded with them, and he made five talents more. So, also, he who had the two talents made two talents more. But he who had received the one talent went and dug in the ground and hid his master's money." (Matthew 25:12-18)

I have lived in fear of this story throughout most of my life because, on some level, I can deeply relate to the servant with one talent. I felt as though what I was given was not enough nor could ever be enough to do something with; I found it easy to watch those around me who have been given more than me, who have access to means, whose minds are full of ideas and who are blessed with the ability to make their life work in their favor. At times, these feelings have caused me to look at myself and see that I don't have their advantages and thus should be content with my average life.

Therefore, I am writing this book as much for myself as I am for whoever is intended to receive this message, in order to prove to myself, my God, and the universe that my fate will not be like the servant with one talent. I will use every fiber of my being to fulfill my purpose, fighting through pain, insecurities, uncertainty, doubt, and a myriad of other emotions because I no longer have the energy to run away. Where has running away from my purpose gotten me? Why do I always resort to the same defense tactics when they have not proven to work in the past? Who am I really afraid of? Why am I afraid to be seen?

These are a few of the questions that I have contemplated over time and no matter what conclusion I arrived at; it was never sufficient. How long will you allow yourself to run away from what's welling up inside of you—begging to be freed, released to the world? Not to bring you fame or glory, but to honor the covenant that you made with the creator in exchange for this mortal experience.

Nothing may ever come of the words that I put to paper. I may be dragged, shamed like the *Song of Ice and Fire* fantasy character, Cersi Lanister, or laughed at by family and friends. Nonetheless, I am pursuing my ultimate legend, and what comes of it will come. When I return to the dust, I want to leave everything I have here in this realm and begin anew. Our purpose is not meant for us to keep to ourselves. It is to provide nourishment for those who are able to digest it and illuminate those who are walking in the darkness of their own journey.

DATING YOUR PURPOSE

During one session, a client began to express frustration with not knowing what their purpose was/is, unsettled by the people around them who seem to have their lives figured out. In my attempt to encourage clients who have been having difficulties in their intimate and interpersonal relationships, I sometimes use the analogy that we need to "date" our purpose. What does that mean, you might ask?

Consider the act of dating. Dating is not marriage; we make no serious life-long commitments to someone we are merely dating. Dating is the fun and exciting exploration phase of meeting someone new. We discover someone we think we might like, plan to meet in person, get dressed up, and attempt to figure out if the two of us might be compatible. Some dates turn into relationships that lead to marriage, while others serve as life lessons for us to contemplate.

The same can be true about our purpose. We flirt with it, try it out, explore the possibilities of what it might be, and make decisions based on the outcome. We ask questions to inquire about intentions, struggle to understand them, contemplate our relationship, and work through difficulties that inevitably arise. Most dates that turn into relationships only happen because we invest the time in the process and the person. We call, text, make plans, and allow ourselves to be vulnerable in the hopes that the person we are dating reciprocates those same feelings.

Our purpose will never reject us; it just may cause us to ask questions of ourselves to make us feel unsure of ourselves. That is the insecurity that we must overcome because purpose does not gaslight us or play tricks, like some of the people we may choose to date. Purpose sees into the depths of our souls and resides in that internal space. It knows our fears, limitations, and the traumas that we have endured. Yet, it asks us questions that challenge these things in order to help us overcome; it is resolute in the fact that despite our faults, it still desires to be a part of our life and journey.

You are the entrepreneur of purpose, and it ain't going to wait for you if you don't work for it!

Your purpose is *your* purpose: It can't live for others. A colleague of mine started a business and asked me to assist. Over the years, he would call on me to help whenever he needed me, and I was always happy to oblige. He eventually asked me what I wanted to do with the company, and I told him I wasn't sure. He expressed that he would love for me to join but said that he did not want to fold my desires for my life into his dream. After sitting with that, I understood exactly what he meant. I knew then that while I enjoyed the work, it was not my dream or my purpose. I was good at it, and I could be a great assistant. But I had to find my own dream and purpose and work vigorously for myself.

ACCEPT THE JOURNEY

"Stay in your lane, but take control of the road."

This adage is often used to express that someone should mind the business that pays them. Some people are woefully unaware that their focus is on what other people are doing while their own work is being neglected. As the expression goes, the grass will always be greener when your hose is used to water others' lawns. Likewise, when people hear the expression "stay in your lane," there is an assumption that the lane is narrow, which causes them to envy the free lanes to their left and right. However, it is important to understand that we are the architects of our lives; we build the roads that we travel, and our lanes can be as wide and expansive as we make them. By putting all of our effort and energy into our own goals, dreams, and purpose, we create limitless opportunities.

To put it another way, it has been said that when we work for others, we work to build their dreams. By focusing on what others are doing, we are pouring life into others while draining ourselves of the sustenance we need to survive. Even negative energy can have the same impact on yourself and others. Haters are often a major motivation for success (yes, I'm calling you a hater!) To look upon others with feelings of jealousy, envy, and strife, you poison your dreams while energizing others to prove a point.

When we come to a place of acceptance and surrender and find peace in our journey, we are able to thrive; our purpose can overflow from a place of positivity. As mentioned frequently in earlier chapters, I thoroughly enjoy watching anime; what stands out to me is that many of the metahumans in these comics and anime start with a basic power. Some grow to resent their gift and never take the time to cultivate the power within. Others choose to accept their limitations and push themselves far beyond what they dreamed they could do (Rock & Guy Lee). Then, there are those born with supernatural abilities that outshine everyone in their path. They are considered geniuses and praised for their inherent gifts. Those who take their gifts for granted begin to look down on others, like Neji, from Naruto, while others appreciate their skill and strive to be the best.

Ultimately, it is up to you to determine who you are and what you want out of life. To seek purpose is to find it, although it may not always look like what you envision. Understand that we are all on a path toward greatness; it is simply up to us to walk it, stand still, or move in the opposite direction. All paths lead to purpose: you just have to *move*.

- Create a list of 3 people you believe have discovered their purpose.
- Read their stories.
- Make a list of themes they all have in common.
- How do you relate to them?
- How do their stories relate to your purpose?

ABOUT THE AUTHOR

I can recall, at a young age, that I had always been drawn to and curious about purpose. I often found myself wondering what I was meant to do. Throughout my journey, I have discovered that my purpose is to help other people discover their own. I can recall many conversations with friends, family, and strangers in which I was able to discern their innate gifts and abilities and work with them to bring out their full potential. These experiences eventually led me to major in psychology as an undergraduate at San Diego State University. During my time there, I discovered a true passion for psychology. I eventually applied to Howard University, where I earned my Ph.D. in clinical psychology in 2019.

While on an internship in Raleigh, North Carolina, in 2018, I was asked to speak to a group of students on a college tour. I created a Life Readiness workshop, where I shared with them some of the aspirational goals of positive psychology. I was inspired to write this book based on that presentation. I discovered that the more I wrote, the clearer it became to me that this was my passion. I began to feel a spark of inspiration every time I talked about writing this book. I started having dreams about it and woke from my sleep many nights to write the words that came to me in my dreams.

This book has been a labor of love for the past few years. I have experienced aspects of every chapter of the book. There were moments when I felt so inspired that I thought I could complete this book in a day; then I started to doubt myself, my abilities, and my purpose. I allowed fear and doubt to take root and slowly began to distance myself from this work, with the fear of being judged or that people would not receive the jewels that I hoped to provide in my writing. As a result, I stopped writing for long periods of time, waiting for inspiration to "hit me," and I refused to do anything until I felt a sensation from some external force. But the longer I waited, the less inspired I became until I decided to move with intention.

I eventually came to the realization that I would have to work through my discomfort, anxiety, and self-doubt to complete this work. After I graduated in 2019, I started working in private practice, seeing up to twenty-five clients a week at the peak of my clinical practice. Most of my clients expressed that they were experiencing some form of anxiety, and at its core, this anxiety was mostly due to not knowing or understanding their purpose.

I realized that I needed to complete this book, even if no one ever bought it or read it. I needed to finish the assignment that I was given. Regardless of the outcome, I will be able to move forward in life knowing that I accomplished my goal.

As you will no doubt become aware throughout the passages of this volume, I have been inspired by *The Alchemist*, an allegorical novel published by Brazilian author Paulo Coelho in 1988. I make it a practice to read it at least once a year. Anytime I find myself in a rut or feeling disconnected from my purpose, I reread it to help me gain clarity in times of uncertainty.

Purpose is a circular definition, meaning that it is difficult to discuss or describe without using the word. I understand that many people may be seeking a singular definition to describe this phenomenon; unfortunately, I cannot provide that. I merely hope that the reader understands that there are myriad pathways to fulfilling it. We must act and move with intentionality, God, the Universe, or whatever force we believe will add wind to our sails.

www.ingramcontent.com/pod-product-compliance
Lightning Source LLC
Chambersburg PA
CBHW051007140626
46546CB00016B/1049